Healing Young People thru Empowerment (H.Y.P.E.):

A Hip-Hop Therapy Program for Black Teenage Boys

Adia McClellan Winfrey, Psy.D.

African American Images

First Edition, First Printing

Front cover illustration by Harold Carr, Jr.

Copyright © 2009 by Adia McClellan Winfrey, Psy.D.

Printed in the United States of America

10-Digit ISBN #: 1-934155-20-9
13-Digit ISBN #: 978-1-934155-20-2

Contents

H.Y.P.E.
(Healing Young People through Empowerment)

Acknowledgments

This project originally began during the first year of my doctoral program as my dissertation. Since that time, its evolution into a curriculum has been a labor of love. The H.Y.P.E. program was born from an impossible dream that I had as a teenager: to utilize hip-hop culture to empower Black adolescents. Through my undergraduate education at Wilberforce University and clinical training at Wright State University School of Professional Psychology, I have been able to push forward and complete this project with support from faculty, direction from my professors, and guidance from my supervisors.

I want to acknowledge Dr. Eugenia Shittu, my advisor and surrogate mom at Wilberforce University, for encouraging me to pursue a doctorate degree in clinical psychology. I must also acknowledge and thank my dissertation committee for encouraging me to go forward with H.Y.P.E. in the early stages when I wasn't sure such a project was possible. Dr. Janeece Warfield, as my dissertation chair/advisor/supervisor, you offered your unconditional support at every level of this project, and I want to acknowledge you for that. In addition, acknowledgments go to Dr. James Dobbins for his guidance and advocacy throughout my journey at SOPP. Finally, Dr. Michael Williams, I want to acknowledge you for the support you provided, encouragement you offered, and the wonderful editorial direction you gave.

I must also recognize two women who truly inspired me to make this dream come true: Toni Blackman and Dr. Lolita Gooden A.K.A. Dr. Roxanne Shante'. These women epitomize hip-hop's richness, and they are living proof that you can live

H.Y.P.E.
(Healing Young People through Empowerment)

an impossible dream. I am looking forward to teaming up with each of you in the near future.

Although my academic experiences undoubtedly impacted the development of this book, I would not have made it this far had it not been for the village that raised me. By the grace of God, I was born into a family of warriors who overcame many obstacles and passed this strength onto their children, their children's children, and then to me. I must recognize my parents, Frank and Juanita McClellan, who provided the various opportunities and offered the guidance necessary to raise a strong Black woman in a racist and sexist society. In addition, I want to acknowledge my brother Kalonji, my sister Angelita, and my only living grandparent, Mrs. Frances Morrow. I also want to shout out all my nephews and nieces and let each of you know that nothing is impossible.

I must also acknowledge my husband, Eric Winfrey, who has been a wonderful father to our children and a good friend to me since Freshman Week at Wilberforce. As I struggled to complete this project, you stepped up and took on parenthood in ways many fathers never will. In addition, I want to acknowledge our children—Donovan, Daymion, Ameerah, and Aidan—for their energy, patience, and beauty.

I must also shout out the youth and staff at Ethan Allen School, where I completed my predoctoral internship and ran my first H.Y.P.E. group. Specifically, I would like to acknowledge Dr. Michael Hagan who supported and believed in me when others doubted the validity of my work. As well, I must acknowledge Dr. Karyn Gust-Brey. She shared her professional expertise in the area of group therapy and boosted my confidence, which helped me feel like a real psychologist! Of course, I can't forget those 17 brave souls who agreed to

Dedications

participate in my very first H.Y.P.E. group. I hope I inspired each of you as much as you inspired me.

Finally, I would like to acknowledge all of those who said a kind word, sent up a prayer, offered encouragement, remained supportive, and always believed in me. You are my family and friends, and I'm blessed to say there are too many of you to name. Just know that without each of your contributions, I am not sure as to whether my journey would have gone like it has. In my darkest hours, your kind thoughts and words uplifted me, and for that I am grateful. As I continue down this path, I feel encouraged to know that each of you are still with me, and remember…we are just getting started!

This work is dedicated to . . .

My children, my children's children, and my children's children's children.

All those who love hip-hop for what it is and what it can be.

All those who have had an impossible dream, whether realized or not.

All Black Americans whose growth and development have been stunted as a result of discrimination and prejudice.

All those leaders who demonized rap music in the '80s, '90s, and '00s, because this led to my interest in advocating for the hip-hop community.

H.Y.P.E.
(Healing Young People through Empowerment)

All the brothers and sisters who have been incarcerated
as a result of racial profiling, unfair sentencing laws,
and lack of opportunity.

All future doctoral psychology students who will use their
dissertations to improve services for Black youth
and their families.

Introduction: The H.Y.P.E. Mission

Black teenage boys are in trouble. In addition to the typical social and psychological changes all teenagers must face, Black adolescent boys are confronted with a unique series of developmental events and psychological responses. Specifically, this group is plagued by shorter life expectancies, higher homicide rates, increasing suicide rates, unequal treatment within the school setting, and they are often criminalized in many sectors of society (Gibbs, 2003). The presence of a mental health disorder may further complicate adolescence for Black boys. However, few curriculums address issues of concern for this group utilizing a culturally relevant approach. The mission of H.Y.P.E. is to provide programming that improves the lives of Black teenage boys with a history of behavior problems, while integrating culturally specific elements.

Several decades ago, the field of psychology was forced to acknowledge the role culture plays in understanding mental health. In following with this acceptance, both Rap Therapy (RT) (Elligan, 2004) and Hip-Hop Therapy (HHT) (Allen, 2005) were developed to offer culturally sensitive approaches to delivering mental health services using rap music. While HHT and RT were conceptually innovative, these programs did not provide detailed facilitative information, specific procedures, group activities, or topics of relevance that should be addressed. In addition, these programs did not provide specific songs or discussion questions, requiring facilitators to rely heavily on the youth they are trying to help. H.Y.P.E. is a 12 session group program

H.Y.P.E.
(Healing Young People through Empowerment)

for use with Black teenage boys and young men between the ages of 13 and 21 that provides details about songs, activities, topics, and includes optional parent and mentor components. In addition, detailed instructions for handouts and activities, process questions for session songs, journal topics, and preparatory session material are included in The Facilitator's Guide (Part 3).

A wide range of individuals are qualified to facilitate H.Y.P.E. While there are no educational requirements, it is imperative that facilitators are able to understand the material included in this book, as well as the collateral information recommended in Part 3. Additionally, facilitators should have experience working with groups of teenagers, in settings that may include church, work, or community organizations. Though group size may vary based on the setting and facilitator preference, it is suggested that groups include six to 10 youth. While H.Y.P.E. member selection will also be impacted by the setting, a number of sources can provide group referrals including family members, neighbors, friends, juvenile corrections employees, church members/preachers, school employees, physicians, mentors, or mental health professionals.

H.Y.P.E. emerged from my lifelong love of hip-hop, recognition of its value in working with young people, and passion for improving the well-being of Black boys. Through using rap music, a genre that has been the voice of Black youth for over 30 years, youth involved in H.Y.P.E. are less defensive and more open to sharing their experiences, while analyzing their pasts and futures.

How to Use This Book

This comprehensive manual includes the literature utilized to develop the H.Y.P.E. program, a detailed outline of the H.Y.P.E. curriculum, a Facilitator's Guide for group implementation, and a Participant's Toolkit (handouts). Because several components are incorporated in this book, all or segments may be utilized in multiple settings by a range of providers, including mental health professionals, youth mentors, and educators, to name a few.

The Literature Supporting the H.Y.P.E. Curriculum section (Part 1) provides readers and potential facilitators a general introduction to the issues plaguing Black teenage boys. Intervention and therapeutic modalities that have been effective with this group are reviewed, and it is this literature that lays the foundation for the H.Y.P.E. program. Whether portions or the entire H.Y.P.E. curriculum will be implemented, it is recommended that facilitators read this section first. The information will enhance understanding of past and current issues salient to Black teenage boys, which can further improve the services provided to this group.

In addition to being used as an intervention tool, the first section of this book in particular can serve as text for a variety of undergraduate and graduate social science or education courses. High school educators may also find this book useful in facilitating discussion among Black students about issues impacting Black America.

In the Healing Young People thru Empowerment Curriculum section (Part 2), the H.Y.P.E. curriculum is introduced, and session details are provided. The goal of this

H.Y.P.E.
(Healing Young People through Empowerment)

section is to make program implementation efficient. This section provides detailed descriptions of the H.Y.P.E. session procedures, themes, objectives, activities, and songs. Each session builds upon the previous ones; thus, the sessions should be delivered in sequential order, particularly if the entire curriculum will be delivered.

It is critical that the Facilitator's Guide (Part 3) be reviewed prior to and during the group sessions. In addition to providing collateral materials that will help with facilitating session activities and group discussion, a consent form, optional pre/posttest test measures, and an outline of the parent/guardian H.Y.P.E. group are included in this section.

The Participant's Toolkit (Part 4) is comprised of H.Y.P.E. session handouts and journal pages.

Facilitators and all others interested in using the H.Y.P.E. curriculum can access the program's website at www.letsgethype.com for session handouts/journal pages, obtain updated program information, request formal H.Y.P.E. training, and to provide general feedback.

It is my hope that you will find this book informative, thought provoking, and useful, whether you use it on your job, in your home, or in your community.

Part 1: Literature Supporting the H.Y.P.E. Curriculum

Chapter 1: Issues Relevant to Black Adolescent Boys

Black adolescent boys are one of the most vulnerable and maltreated groups in this society (Gibbs, 2003). They have been victims of miseducation within the school system, inequality within the juvenile justice system, mislabeled by mental health agencies, neglected by the social welfare system, and have even been labeled an "endangered species." This has led to high rates of psychological and behavioral disorders, in addition to problematic psychosocial behaviors (Gibbs, 2003). Although various factors may be attributed to these trends, historic dynamics are a part of the equation and should be examined (Gibbs, 2003; Taylor et al., 1997).

Some historical events that have contributed negatively to the experiences of many Black adolescent boys include slavery, segregation and discrimination, poverty, and urbanization (Gibbs, 2003). Although widely debated, a general impact of slavery was the destabilization of the family structure, which paralleled the demise of the man as the head of household. Even when slavery was abolished, families were forever separated, and the foundation for family structure was established. The following 100 years in America were marked by segregation that created a "separate but unequal" society and treated Black Americans as second-class citizens (Gibbs, 2003). Segregation forced many Black youth to attend substandard primary and secondary schools, denied them admission to many colleges, and generally attempted to place a limit on the future Black youth believed they could have. This system required parents to design childrearing strategies that would enable their children to develop in a healthy manner.

H.Y.P.E.
(Healing Young People through Empowerment)

Income level has also impacted the status of Black adolescents, with Black families being three times more likely to be poor than White families. Income level is usually a deciding factor in where a person lives, the school children attend, and much more (Gibbs, 2003).

Finally, the migration of Black Americans from the South to the North between World Wars I and II led to the development of huge "ghettos." This led to a concentration of Black males with few industrial opportunities, increased social and cultural isolation from the dominant society, and eventually an "underclass" that can still be seen several generations later. Today, many of the biggest problems Black adolescent boys face are directly related to these historical events. Two related issues are poor education and elevated dropout rates (Gibbs, 2003).

The high school dropout rate for Black adolescents is close to 25 percent, which is about 11 percent higher than the national average (Mishel & Joydeep, 2006). However, in some of the largest cities in the U.S. (e.g., New York City and Chicago), the number is as high as 70 percent (Jackson, 2005). Those lacking a high school education have few job opportunities. Many Black adolescent boys seek alternative means of earning money, including anti-social and even criminal behaviors to survive (Hoke, 2006). The pool of poorly educated Black males is becoming even more disconnected from the mainstream society and to a far greater degree than comparable White or Latino males.

Over-representation in the juvenile court system is also a relevant issue within this group. In 2000, the total delinquency case rate for Black adolescents was more than twice that of White adolescents and nearly three times that of youth of other races (Office of Juvenile Justice and Delinquency Prevention,

Chapter 1: Issues Relevant to Black Adolescent Boys

2000). Additionally, whereas Black youth made up about 16 percent of the juvenile population in 2000, they constituted 42 percent of all juvenile arrests (U.S. Department of Justice, Office of Justice Programs, Office of Juvenile Justice and Prevention, 2000).

Similarly disproportionate disciplinary consequence rates are found in the school environment among Black adolescents and those of other races (Indiana Education Policy Center, 2000). Black students are more likely to be suspended and expelled, suffering harsher consequences for behavioral problems than their White peers. During the 1999–2000 school year, Black students with disabilities were more than three times as likely as White students to be given short-term suspensions. Similarly, they were nearly three times more likely than White students to be removed from school for more than ten days (http://www.childrensdefense.org/site/DocServer/idea.pdf).

Family structure is another cause for concern. In 2003, it was reported that 76 percent of Black children did not live with their fathers. Rodney and Mupier (1999) investigated the impact father absence has on Black boys with a sample that included subjects who lived with and without their fathers. The data revealed that those with absent fathers were more likely to be retained in a grade, to skip a grade due to poor behavior, run away from home, and be suspended from school. It should be noted that Black children are more likely to reside in the home of a grandparent than are White or Latino children (Taylor et al., 1997). This presents a unique dynamic that must be addressed when studying the Black family, and it underscores the importance of extended family in Black culture.

3

H.Y.P.E.
(Healing Young People through Empowerment)

Researchers have investigated the role environment plays in the development and well-being of Black children and adolescents. According to DeCarlo and Hockman (2001), 80 percent of all Black children and adolescents live in "distressed" communities. Distressed communities have been characterized by high mobility, high population density, substandard housing, family dysfunction, high unemployment, poverty, and "slum like" conditions (Joseph, 1999). Members of distressed communities are often ignored by mainstream society and are offered few resources to improve their living situations. Residents in these underserved areas may experience feelings of despair, powerlessness, and social alienation as a result of these conditions (Joseph, 1999). Urban ecologists have suggested that such physical and social environments can promote deviant behavior, including crime and delinquency. Residing in such a neighborhood also increases one's likelihood of being both the victim and perpetrator of a violent crime (Joseph, 1999).

Jarjoura, Triplett, and Brinker (2002) studied the connection between poverty and delinquency. Fourteen waves of the National Longitudinal Survey of Youth (NYSY) data, from 1979 to 1992, were used in this analysis. A measure of the percent of the youth's life spent in poverty was constructed to adjust for age. "Poverty spells," which indicated the longest continuous period (in years) that the youth's family lived in poverty, were also measured. Delinquency was operationalized as the number of times each youth reported engaging in each of the following six behaviors: hurting someone badly enough to need a doctor, taking something without paying for it, damaging school property on purpose, getting drunk, skipping

4

school without permission, or staying out one night without permission. The measure of self-reported delinquency was regressed on each of the measures of poverty, and the researchers found that poverty is significantly related to higher levels of involvement in self-reported delinquency. Furthermore, Jarjoura et al. found that as the longest continuous period in poverty increased, so did the likelihood of reporting a higher level of involvement in delinquency. Thus the authors found that a significant connection between poverty and delinquency exists.

Lower stages of racial identity development may impact the involvement of Black adolescents in anti-social behavior as well. Black racial identity can be defined as the developmental process by which a person "becomes Black." This concept has been influenced largely by Cross's Nigrescence theory (1971). In this theory, "Black" is defined as a psychological connection with one's race rather than the identification of one's skin color (Cross, 1971; Plummer, 1995). Cross's original model has been revised several times. However, the original version includes the following four stages: Pre-encounter, Encounter, Immersion-Emersion, and Internalization (Cross, 1971).

Those within the Pre-Encounter stage of racial identity development display one of three attitudes toward their race: low-salience, social stigma, or anti-Black. Those experiencing low-salience do not deny being Black; however, their blackness plays an insignificant role in their daily lives, their well-being, or the manner in which they define themselves. Those with the social stigma attitude view themselves as Black by default (they just happen to be Black)—and they are ashamed of this fact. Individuals possessing the anti-Black attitude view their racial status as negative; they feel estranged from other Black people and the Black community. Each of these attitudes yields favoritism towards all things European or White, including beauty, relationships, art, and communication style (Cross, 1971).

Encounter, the second stage of this model, involves an evolution in identity brought on by a major event or series of events (encounter) that lead to cognitive dissonance. The encounter causes the individual to question pre-encounter beliefs and attitudes, leading to his/her increased awareness of racial status in America. Along with this awareness comes guilt, anger, uncertainty, and confusion about one's level of "blackness." Individuals in this stage tend to spend a lot of time trying to find a positive Black identity by gathering information from various sources (e.g., media outlets, books, and relationships with other Black people) (Cross, 1971; Ford & Harris, 1997).

The third stage of this model, Immersion-Emersion, is divided into two sub-areas. Those in the Immersion phase are trying to become the "right" kind of Black person, and they identify anything White as evil and oppressive. Feelings of rage and pride are dominant during this phase. During the Emersion phase, the anti-White attitudes and idealistic thoughts about "blackness" eventually decline. These are substituted for a deeper investigation of issues impacting Black people, such as economic disparities and disproportionately high incarceration rates (Cross, 1971; Ford & Harris, 1997).

Internalization, the final stage of this model, is characterized by an appreciation of multiculturalism while remaining "true"

6

Chapter 1: Issues Relevant to Black Adolescent Boys

to one's "blackness." The individual is better able to defend and protect the ego from psychological problems and stress associated with living in a racist society. Additional outcomes of this stage include gaining a basis for interacting in situations with non-Black individuals and a sense of belonging (Cross, 1971; Ford & Harris, 1997).

Cross asserts that one can regress, progress, or remain stagnant at any stage along this continuum. He did not place age constraints on this theory, so a 14-year-old and a 40-year-old can have the same level of racial identity. He did, however, suggest that one's personality, social support, resources, and experiences heavily influence how one progresses through the stages of this model (Worrell et. al, 2001).

Several studies have investigated the impact of racial identity on other areas of functioning among Black adolescents (Ford & Harris, 1997; McCreary et al., 1996). In 1996, McCreary, Slavin, and Berry explored the notion that racial identity can act as a buffer to problem behavior. The authors utilized the National Survey of Black Americans: Group and Personal Identity Scale (Jackson, Tucker, & Gurin, 1987) to measure the subjects' "African-American attitudes" that were based on their endorsements of positive and negative stereotypes about Black people. They found that African-American attitudes were related inversely and significantly to problem behavior among adolescents; thus the "higher" the African-American attitude the lower the incidence of problem behavior. Miller (1999) also explored the impact of negative feelings about Black people on Black adolescents. He found that such thinking

H.Y.P.E.
(Healing Young People through Empowerment)

leads to a depreciated character, a sense of worthlessness and inadequacy, and a devaluation of self. Furthermore, such an individual will be more likely to turn away from positive societal norms and expectations.

Chapter 2: Descriptions of Mental Health Diagnoses Addressed in H.Y.P.E.

Delinquency in Black adolescent boys is often accompanied by a DSM-IV-TR diagnosis of Conduct Disorder, Attention Deficit Hyperactivity Disorder, and/or Oppositional Defiant Disorder (Grisso, Davis, & Vincent, 2004). Additionally, these diagnoses may each be classified as Severe Emotional Disorders, Emotional or Behavioral Disorders, and/or Disruptive Behavior Disorders, each of which will be described in this section.

Conduct Disorder

Conduct Disorder is a repetitive pattern of behavior in children and adolescents in which the rights of others or basic societal rules are violated. Children and adolescents with this diagnosis usually exhibit severe aggressive and antisocial acts that interfere with the rights of others. These acts include physical and verbal aggression, stealing, or committing acts of vandalism (Erik, 2004). This behavior pattern occurs in a variety of settings (e.g., at home, at school, and in social situations) and causes significant impairment in the individual's social, academic, and family functioning (Erik, 2004).

The prevalence rate for this disorder runs from one to ten percent. The following are characteristics and behaviors exhibited by adolescents with Conduct Disorder:
1. Aggressive behavior that causes or threatens harm to other people or animals, such as bullying or intimidating others,

initiating physical fights, or being physically cruel to animals;

2. Non-aggressive conduct that causes property loss or damage, such as fire-setting or the deliberate destruction of property;

3. Deceitfulness or theft, such as breaking into someone's house or car, lying, or "conning" others; and

4. Serious rule violations, such as staying out at night when prohibited, running away from home overnight, or often being truant from school (American Psychiatric Association, 2000; Erik, 2004).

Many youth who have been diagnosed with Conduct Disorder have trouble feeling and expressing empathy or remorse and reading social cues. These youth often misinterpret the actions of others as being hostile or aggressive and respond by escalating the situation into conflict (Erik, 2004). A Conduct Disorder diagnosis may also be associated with other difficulties, such as substance use, risk-taking behavior, school problems, and physical injury from accidents or fights (American Psychiatric Association, 2000). Additionally, adolescents from urban areas have higher rates of Conduct Disorder diagnoses than those from rural areas (Erik, 2004).

Attention Deficit Hyperactivity Disorder (ADHD)

ADHD is a neurobehavioral disorder characterized by developmentally inappropriate degrees of inattention, impulsivity, and/or hyperactivity resulting in significant functional impairment. ADHD was first recognized as a legitimate disorder more than a century ago. The reported prevalence rate of ADHD ranges from 1.7 to 17.8 percent. These variations are likely due to multiple interpretations of the diagnostic criteria, differences among informant reports, and cultural factors. The estimated incidence in school-age children by DSM-IV-T-R criteria is about 10 percent (Department of Continuing Medical Education, 1999).

For a diagnosis of ADHD to be given, signs of hyperactivity, impulsivity, and/or inattention must have been present for at least six months. The following are symptoms commonly displayed by those with an ADHD diagnosis:

1. Often does not give close attention to details or makes careless mistakes on school assignments, at work, or when doing other activities;
2. Often has trouble keeping attention on tasks or play activities;
3. Often does not seem to listen when spoken to directly;
4. Often fidgets with hands or feet or squirms in seat;
5. Often gets up from seat when remaining seated is expected;
6. Often blurts out answers before questions have been finished; and
7. Often has trouble waiting one's turn (American Psychiatric Association, 2000).

Oppositional Defiant Disorder (ODD)

ODD is a recurring pattern of negative, hostile, disobedient, and defiant behavior in a child or adolescent that lasts for at least six months without serious violation of the basic rights of others. The behavioral disturbances cause clinically significant problems in social, school, or work functioning. Those with this disorder display an age-inappropriate pattern of stubborn, hostile, and defiant behavior that may be exhibited as early as preschool or kindergarten (Erik, 2004). These behaviors have been shown to have negative and/or reciprocal effects on parent-child and teacher-student relationships. Those with an ODD diagnosis may be unwilling to compromise, give in, or negotiate with adults. Some behaviors commonly exhibited by adolescents diagnosed with ODD include the following:

1. Loses temper often;
2. May deliberately annoy people;
3. Blames others for his or her mistakes or misbehavior;
4. Is often angry and resentful; and
5. Can be spiteful or vindictive (American Psychiatric Association, 2000).

ODD has a prevalence rate ranging from 2 to 16 percent and usually becomes evident before eight years of age, but not later than adolescence. However, among low income families, the prevalence rate for meeting the DSM criteria for ODD can run as high as three-quarters of clinic-referred preschoolers (Erik, 2004).

Disruptive Behavior Disorders (DBDs)

DBDs are the most common reasons children are referred to mental health practitioners for possible treatment. "Disruptive Behavior Disorders" is an umbrella term that encompasses the specific disorders of CD, ODD, and ADHD. Research has identified both biological and environmental causes of DBD (Erik, 2004). Youth most at risk for ODD and CD are those who have low birth weight, neurological damage, or ADHD. Individuals may also be at risk if they were rejected by their mothers as babies, separated from their parents, given poor foster care, physically or sexually abused, raised in homes with mothers who were abused, or living in poverty (Erik, 2004).

DBDs are of great concern to this society due to the high degree of behavioral impairment and poor prognosis that accompany them (Erik, 2004). They often lead to a lifetime of social dysfunctions, antisocial behavior patterns, and poor adjustment.

Severe Emotional Disorder

A Severe Emotional Disorder (SED) is defined under the Individuals with Disabilities Act (IDEA) as a condition with one or more of the following characteristics (must be present over a long period of time and to a marked degree, adversely affecting educational performance):

1. An inability to learn that cannot be explained by intellectual, sensory, or health factors;
2. An inability to build or maintain satisfactory interpersonal relationships with peers and teachers;
3. Inappropriate behaviors or feelings under normal circumstances;
4. A general pervasive mood of unhappiness or depression; or
5. A tendency to develop physical symptoms or fears associated with personal or school problems (Erik, 2004).

The SED label does not refer to a specific psychiatric disorder, but rather is a legal definition that allows a child meeting these criteria to receive special education services.

H.Y.P.E.
(Healing Young People through Empowerment)

Determination of an SED must be made by a multi-disciplinary team that includes input from parents as well as professionals. The following are examples of diagnoses that may accompany an SED label: mood disorders, anxiety disorders, disruptive behavior disorders, and pervasive developmental disorders (Erik, 2004). Grisso, Davis, & Vincent (2004) reported that about 15 to 20 percent of youth in pre-trial detention and correctional programs are classified as SED.

Emotional or Behavioral Disorders (EBD)

EBD refers to a condition in which the behavioral or emotional responses of an individual in a school setting are so different from age appropriate, ethnic, or cultural norms that performance in areas such as self care, social relationships, personal adjustment, academic progress, classroom behavior, or work adjustment is adversely affected (NASP, 2006). EBD is more than a transient, expected response to stressors in the adolescent's environment and may persist even with individualized interventions (e.g., feedback to the individual, consultation with parents or families, and/or modification of the educational environment). This category may include schizophrenia, affective disorders, anxiety disorders, or other sustained disturbances of behavior, emotions, attention, or adjustment (Erik, 2004). The impact of the behavior on the student's educational progress must be the guiding principle for identification. Despite the varying types of emotional disorders, children with EBD often have the following similar characteristics: generally being male (White or Black), hyperactive, aggressive, withdrawn, immature, and from a "non-traditional" home environment (e.g., single-parent household or foster care).

Chapter 3: Methods Historically Used to Treat Adolescents with Disruptive Behavior Disorders

A variety of methods have been employed to treat adolescents with Disruptive Behavior Disorders, including group, individual, family, and music therapies. More recently, Rap Therapy and Hip-Hop Therapy have been utilized in interventions with Black adolescents and young adults who are dealing with a variety of disorders. Each of these approaches will be explored in this section.

Group vs. Individual Therapy

When designing an intervention for Black adolescent boys with significant behavioral problems, the appropriateness of individual versus group therapy immediately arises as a concern. Shechtman (2003) compared the outcomes and processes of group and individual treatment with 102 aggressive boys.

Therapeutic outcomes were measured using the Group Counseling Helpful Impacts Scales (GCHIS), which contain the following components: Emotional Awareness-Insight, Relationship-Climate, Other versus Self-focus, and Problem Identification-Change. Shechtman (2003) found that although the therapeutic outcomes were unremarkable for three of the four components when comparing group and individual therapy, Emotional Awareness-Insight was significantly greater with group therapy participants. Additionally, Problem Identification-Change showed a linear slope, which suggests that over time, growth occurred in this domain for group participants. This may have been due to the developmental

H.Y.P.E.
(Healing Young People through Empowerment)

needs of children and adolescents and the fact that group cohesiveness, catharsis, and developing socialization skills are crucial for this age group.

Corbin (1994) suggested that group therapy is a very effective mode of therapy for several reasons. First, it emphasizes egalitarian relationships and interactions that counter the lopsided authority in individual therapy. This may prove important when working with a population that feels powerless. Additionally, it provides children and adolescents with a peer-focused environment to share their experiences, thoughts, and feelings. It also provides them with problem-solving strategies, knowledge, and immediate practice in initiating and sustaining prosocial relations (DeCarlo & Hockman, 2003).

Group therapy is the most common modality for treatment offered to children and adolescents in published outcome studies, which include treatments for anger management and conduct problems. A primary indication for group therapy is that the presenting problem is interpersonal in nature. Common presenting problems include social inhibition, impulse-control problems, social-skills deficits, chronic interpersonal conflicts, and the need for social support. However, it should be noted that groups may be less appropriate for habitually antisocial youth, possibly serving as "deviancy training" and increasing the participants' negative behaviors. This has been particularly true in groups involving younger adolescents (DeCarlo & Hockman, 2003).

Individual therapy is generally warranted if the adolescent is in crisis, the problem is based on intrapsychic conflict, and the nature of the problem is intimate or specific. This form of therapy is also beneficial if the client is not suitable for group therapy due to his or her developmental stage or psychiatric diagnosis (Shechtman, 2003).

Chapter 3: Methods Historically Used to Treat Adolescents with Disruptive Behavior Disorders

Family Therapy

Family therapy is an important modality for Black youth because parental communication and support are essential to the successful resolution of obstacles they may face. It is especially appropriate for Black adolescent boys who are delinquent or predelinquent, depressed, suicidal, "scapegoated," or if a breakdown in family communication exists (Gibbs, 2003).

Successful family therapy with Black families often includes an eclectic blend of structural and strategic techniques, such as restructuring the family roles, modifying family communication, and changing social behaviors. Multisystemic therapy is also effective with Black adolescents involved in the juvenile court system (Gibbs, 2003). Since many teenagers are struggling to separate from their families and to function independently, the clinician must make a careful assessment of the advantages and disadvantages of family therapy for a given client (Gibbs, 2003).

Music Therapy

Music therapy has been used for centuries in the areas of healing and education (DeCarlo & Hockman, 2003). In the past few decades, models of music therapy have been based on various theoretical backgrounds, including psychodynamic, behavioral, and humanistic orientations. When utilizing a psychodynamic orientation, the most prominent models of music therapy are Analytical Music Therapy (AMT) and Guided Imagery and Music (GIM). AMT involves free improvisation using symbolically expressed inner moods and associations, while GIM entails listening to recorded music

H.Y.P.E.
(Healing Young People through Empowerment)

as a way of bringing up inner images to be reflected upon (Darnley-Smith & Patey, 2003). Humanistic models of music therapy focus on improvisations dealing with "here and now" experiences to foster emotional awareness. Creative Music Therapy and Orff Music Therapy, both used with a humanistic model, focus on improvisation in a more structured form than used with a psychodynamic model. Behavioral Music Therapy is based on Skinner's behaviorist theory and uses various forms of playing and singing music, as well as listening to music as a conditional reinforcement or stimulus cue to modify behavior (Darnley-Smith & Patey, 2003). There are also eclectic models that combine more than one theoretical background (Gold et. al, 2004).

In general, adolescents can benefit from the use of music therapy in group interventions because it provides a safe, nonthreatening outlet for expressing emotions, and this facilitates the therapeutic process. Music therapy groups may also help participants learn appropriate social skills as a result of interactions and feedback from the facilitators and other members (Saroyan, 1990; & Allen, 2005).

Gold et. al (2004) conducted a meta-analysis of 11 studies that sought to determine the overall efficacy of music therapy for children and adolescents with psychopathology. The impact of pathology, age, music therapy approach, and type of outcome were compared. The analysis revealed that the nonjudgmental nature of this form of therapy had a beneficial effect on children diagnosed with developmental or behavioral disorders. Additionally, an eclectic approach was also found to have been the most effective, yet it was encouraged that the therapist be mindful of each child's strengths and needs. Behavioral models of music therapy tended to yield smaller effects than other approaches. However, when the therapeutic focus was on overt behavior, change effects were larger.

Chapter 4: Hip-Hop, Hip-Hop Therapy, and Rap Therapy

Hip-hop culture emerged in the Bronx, New York, in the early 1970's. The four elements of hip-hop are graffiti art, break dancing, djing (using two turntables and records to create a new sound), and rapping. Rap music was created by Black and Latino youth in the Bronx after music programs were removed from area public schools. With the help of DJ Kool Herc, who emigrated to the U.S. from Jamaica in the 1960's, rap emerged as an opportunity for the disenfranchised to express themselves. Because he introduced the Jamaican tradition of rapping over a beat with two turntables, he is commonly regarded as the godfather of rap. By 1979, the first rap song, "Rapper's Delight" by the Sugar Hill Gang, was recorded, and rap music soon became a national success. Like the blues and rock-n-roll before it, rap music was a genre embraced by young Black culture—and misunderstood by mainstream society.

Despite this fact, rap music is one of the most popular forms of music among young people in America, and it has influenced every facet of U.S. culture, from advertising to language to fashion (Tyson, 2002). Among Black adolescent boys, 97 percent report "liking" rap music, and more than 50 percent report buying at least one new CD a month (Tyson, 2002). The fact that the majority of rap and hip-hop artists are also Black males likely adds to the appeal of the art form among this group in that the artists personalize their own stories (Elligan, 2000). Hip-hop is also international; thriving hip-hop scenes can be found in countries all over the world, particularly in regions where people are disenfranchised. It

H.Y.P.E.
(Healing Young People through Empowerment)

has exceeded all boundaries of race, nationality, language, socioeconomic status, and any other demographic one can imagine. As a result, hip-hop is a multi-billion dollar industry (Tyson, 2002).

The previous research on rap music (Johnson et. al, 1995) has been highly limited, primarily focusing on negative outcomes that result when one "consumes" rap music. This and other studies have attempted to show a correlation among antisocial behavior, rap music, and videos. Much of the backlash directed towards rap music, rap artists, and hip-hop culture in general has been fueled by outspoken politicians (including Presidential candidates and Senators), political activists, and religious leaders who disapprove of the content in some songs (Dyson, 1996). Recently, however, more literature has been published supporting rap music, its ability to empower listeners, and its role in culturally sensitive interventions (Mickel & Mickel, 2002; Tyson, 2002).

Hip-Hop Therapy

HHT is a groundbreaking combination of rap music, bibliotherapy, and music therapy (Tyson, 2002). By analyzing rap lyrics, discussion is generated as participants' life experiences and struggles are examined. Additionally, issues involving social, environmental, and political factors can be addressed (Allen, 2005).

HHT is designed and best utilized as an engagement tool in psychotherapeutic or educational settings for high-risk youth and young adults. This form of therapy addresses issues pertinent to a population that has been overlooked by traditional forms of therapy (Allen, 2005). It may also allow

20

Chapter 4: Hip-Hop, Hip-Hop Therapy, and Rap Therapy

practitioners to connect with youth more effectively by displaying a level of openness to learning from their perspective and exploring lyrics with them (Tyson, 2002).

HHT can be used in a group or individual therapy setting as well as on a long-term or short-term basis. Because a variety of topics are covered within rap music, therapy can be extremely diverse; therefore it is necessary to consider the type of rap music the participants are fond of (Elligan, 2000; Allen, 2005; Mickel & Mickel, 2002).

Using Allen's model (2005), a hip-hop therapist should follow these listed procedures when utilizing the Hip-Hop Therapy model within a group intervention:

1. *Complete an assessment.* Review the clients' presenting issues, investigate their interest in hip-hop, and obtain their psychosocial histories.
2. *Plan icebreaker activities.* Ease tension within the group and establish rapport. This can be done by playing parts of rap songs and having the clients guess the artists.
3. *Establish HHT group guidelines.* This procedure is also interactive in that the therapist can give each group member the opportunity to suggest a rule.
4. *Assemble materials and resources.* These can include a CD player, rap music CDs, copies of the lyrics, and notebooks for journaling. Additionally, music videos and movies may be utilized.
5. *Prepare.* The therapist should examine the music and lyrics prior to the session to become more familiar with the artists' messages and the relevance of the songs to the issues addressed within the group.
6. *Establish HHT learning objectives.* The therapist should use the information obtained during Procedure 1 as a tool

H.Y.P.E.
(Healing Young People through Empowerment)

to develop the learning objectives while also considering group dynamics.

7. *Set goals.* Develop and implement goals for each client.

8. *Encourage journal writing.* This procedure is optional; however, journal writing gives group members the opportunity to express themselves in a private manner. If this part of the model is used, the therapist should make comments in each person's journal entries at the end of each session. Clients can also use journals to create their own lyrics.

9. *Facilitate discussion.* Encourage client feedback through journal entries, which often leads them to share their own stories.

10. *Intervene.* Deconstruct the negative behaviors of group members (as well as behaviors that may be inferred in the lyrics) while introducing positive healthy behaviors. The therapist should also concentrate on validating the clients' feelings and opinions during this phase.

11. *Facilitate a closing activity.* At the end of each session, group members should summarize what they have learned and/or experienced in the group.

Outcome research with this method of group therapy is almost nonexistent; however, Tyson (2002) used a pretest-posttest experimental design with at-risk and delinquent youth at a residential facility to compare the outcomes of HHT and comparison group therapy. Eleven subjects were divided into either the HHT group (n=5) or comparison group (n=6). The HHT group was comprised of two Black males, one White male, one Latino male, and one Latino female, with a mean age of 15.4 years. The comparison group included two Black males, one Latino male, two Black females, and one White female, with a mean age of 16.2 years. The measures used in this study were the Self-Concept Scale for Children and the Index of Peer Relations Scale.

Following their participation in the assigned group, a posttest was given to the HHT participants. The analysis did not indicate a significant difference between the groups when controlling for pretest scores. However, during the debriefing, the HHT participants reported that they enjoyed the group experience more than any they had participated in previously, indicating an appreciation for the "respect" paid to "their" music. Although no significant differences were found in the pretest and posttest scores between groups, it was opinioned that a study including a larger sample would be necessary before conclusions can be made about the effectiveness of HHT.

Rap Therapy

Elligan (2004) developed the Rap Therapy approach as an individual therapy modality. This approach is comprised of five phases and can be used with adolescents and young adults who like rap music and identify with hip-hop culture. The phases are:

1. *Assess and plan.* Assess the client's interest in rap music and hip-hop culture while developing a plan for using rap music with the individual.
2. *Build an alliance.* Talk to the client about rap songs he enjoys to build a relationship and alliance with him.
3. *Reframe thoughts and behaviors.* Use the client's favorite rap lyrics to challenge him to reevaluate his thoughts and behaviors.

H.Y.P.E.
(Healing Young People through Empowerment)

4. *Reinforce through writing.* Have the client write songs (raps) about the desired change that was set as a goal.
5. *Maintain the change.* Monitor and maintain the client's progress through continued discussions and feedback (Elligan, 2004).

Chapter 5: Issues Salient to Black Adolescent Boys with Disruptive Behavior Disorder (DBD)

Historically, Black men have not been granted privilege or power in the United States. Social, cultural, and economic forces manifested in racism and oppression throughout American history have hindered many Black men from assuming culturally accepted masculine roles.

The persistence of such barriers to the achievement and expression of manhood has negatively hindered the mastery of crucial adolescent developmental tasks for many Black boys (Lee, 1996). Racism, socioeconomic disadvantages, and extreme environmental stress often converge to negatively impact the development of Black children during the early, critical years of life. Thus it is not unusual for Black boys to reach adolescence with a basic mistrust of their environment, doubts about their abilities, confusion about their place in the world, and extreme behavioral difficulties (Lee, 1996; Caldwell & White, 2001).

These impediments to adolescent development can often be seen in negative and self-destructive values, attitudes, and behaviors among this young population. The result has been academic underachievement, unemployment, delinquency, substance abuse, homicide, and disproportionate incarceration for Black adolescent boys (Lee, 1996). The following seven issues have been identified as relevant to Black adolescent boys with DBD diagnoses and are addressed in the H.Y.P.E. curriculum (Denham & Almeida, 1987; Lee, 1996; Kellner & Bry, 1999; Caldwell & White, 2001; Dubois et al., 2002; Parham, 2002; Boyd-Franklin, 2003; Gibbs, 2003):

H.Y.P.E.
(Healing Young People through Empowerment)

1. Family participation in the process;
2. Racial identity development;
3. Interpersonal cognitive problem-solving difficulties;
4. Inadequate anger management skills;
5. Difficulty in the school environment;
6. Poor self-concept; and
7. Lack of mentorship opportunities.

Family Participation in the Process

The family is the most important influence in the lives of children and the first line of defense against delinquency. Additionally, research indicates that perceived parental involvement contributes positively to the psychological well-being of adolescents. Thus the role of a strong and positive adult influence appears to be important to an adolescent's evolving self-concept (Joseph, 1999; Gibson & Jefferson, 2006). Unfortunately, one of the greatest challenges when intervening with high-risk Black boys is working effectively with their families. Discomfort with the mental health system, guilt, and exclusively focusing on the child's behavior have been identified as barriers to working with some Black families (Boyd-Franklin, 2003; Nakashian & Kleinman, 1999; Hines & Boyd-Franklin, 1996).

Racial Identity

Race has powerful implications for personality development and mental health. Given the central role of race in American history and sociopolitical life, the developmental processes and life paths of all Americans are affected by race.

Chapter 5: Issues Salient to Black Adolescent Boys with Disruptive Behavior Disorders (DBD)

Overall, racial identity theories suggest that a person's race is more than his or her skin color or physical features, and people's racial identities vary by the extent to which they identify with their respective racial groups (Parham, 2002). Additionally, racial identity theories (Cross, 1971; Parham, 2002) postulate that a person's resolution of his or her identity is crucial because it seems to guide an individual's feelings, thoughts, perceptions, and level of investment in his or her racial groups' cultural patterns (Sanchez & Carter, 2005).

Black racial identity has been cited as a crucial component of a Black American's personality development, and as previously mentioned, may impact the presence of delinquency among Black adolescents (Cross, 1971; Ford & Harris, 1997; Plummer, 1996; Worrell et al., 2001). In addition, other researchers have found that racial identity may impact academic achievement.

Ford and Harris (1997) examined the relationship between student racial identity and school achievement among 152 Black students in grades six to nine in five Mid-Atlantic public school districts. The comparisons were made using the variables of gender, achievement status (underachieving vs. achieving), and academic ability (gifted, potentially gifted, and general education). Regarding academic ability, these researchers found that gifted students had the highest level of racial identity (internalization) of the three groups. Additionally, male underachievers had a significantly lower mean on the internalization subscale than male achievers. Ford and Harris also found that a disproportionately high percentage of the more than 40 percent of students that were underachieving, were also male and in general education classes. The researchers suggest that talking to Black boys in

H.Y.P.E.
(Healing Young People through Empowerment)

small groups about issues of race and associated low teacher expectations, among other things, may help to curve the high incidence of underachievement regardless of the ability level.

Difficulty in the School Environment

The school as an instrument of education and socialization has long been a source of conflict and controversy for Black children and adolescents. Black adolescents may respond to these dysfunctional surroundings with apathy, alienation, hostility, anxiety, by acting out, or identifying with the antisocial elements within the school (Gibbs, 2003). This group is frequently referred for school-related academic or behavioral problems, and it may be a clinician's task to separate an adolescent's presenting problems from the environmental factors that may have exacerbated them (Gibbs, 2003).

As a result of these difficulties, Black boys have been disproportionately affected by the increased emphasis on discipline that occurs in large school settings. The trend throughout the 1990's toward "get-tough" approaches to violence disproportionately affected Black boys (Roderick, 2005). High schools are too often environments in which Black boys are marginalized and unsupported, thus decreasing their motivation and sending them messages that undermine a positive sense of competence and efficacy in school settings (Roderick, 2005).

Black students are also overrepresented in special education programs and nonacademic tracks. Often mislabeled in elementary school, many Black adolescents either drop out or are "pushed out" of high school after experiencing years of academic failure, low achievement, low teacher expectations, high rates of suspension, and chaotic school environments (Gibbs, 2003). If clinicians suspect that students are performing below their abilities, they should intervene. If a discrepancy is discovered between an adolescent's potential ability and the elements of the educational setting, a recommendation for a more appropriate academic placement could be extremely effective (Gibbs, 2003).

Interpersonal Cognitive Problem-Solving

The Interpersonal Cognitive Problem-Solving (ICPS) theory of behavior predicts that children who have a number of alternative ICPS skills to draw from can be more flexible in choosing solutions to social conflicts, are less likely to act impulsively, and are more likely to act appropriately in social situations. Some examples of ICPS skills include:

1. The ability to generate a number of alternative solutions to a conflict;
2. The ability to choose and implement an appropriate solution to a conflict; and
3. Understanding and considering the social consequences of one's actions for oneself and others (Denham & Almeida, 1987).

Without these skills, adolescents are more likely to have frustrating social encounters. This frustration, in turn, can cause adolescents to misbehave, therefore feeding into the cycle of unpleasant social interactions, hurt feelings, frustration, and bad behaviors (www.psychologymatters.org/shure.html).

H.Y.P.E.
(Healing Young People through Empowerment)

Anger Management

Perhaps no greater challenge faces the clinical and educational communities than helping troubled adolescents learn to cope with angry feelings in a socially appropriate manner. A growing number of researchers are addressing the needs of such adolescents in a variety of outpatient, public school, and institutional settings by building cognitive-behavioral skills (Kellner & Bry, 1999). Their treatment efforts have included individual, group, and psychoeducational group modalities. This research suggests that through these interventions, adolescents have acquired anger management skills and exhibited a reduction in the frequency and intensity of acting-out behaviors (Kellner & Bry, 1999).

Deffenbacher, Lynch, Oetting, and Kemper (1996) have also investigated treatment specificity and efficacy. Anger-prone early adolescents attending regular schools, who were taught either cognitive coping skills or social skills, showed a reduction in inappropriate anger expression and an increase in controlled anger expression. Further, Nugent, Champlin, and Winimaki (1997) reported positive results when anger control techniques were taught to delinquent adolescents in a group home setting. In fact, they found that the longer the duration of training, the greater the reduction in antisocial, acting-out behavior.

According to Feindler and Ecton (1986), anger management training typically includes the following:
1. Providing information on the cognitive and behavioral components of anger;
2. Teaching cognitive and behavioral techniques to manage anger; and

Chapter 5: Issues Salient to Black Adolescent Boys with Disruptive Behavior Disorders (DBD)

3. Facilitating the application of newly acquired skills. Specific skills, such as relaxation, assertiveness, self-instruction, self-evaluation, role-play, and problem solving, are emphasized. In addition, participants are often encouraged to document anger-provoking situations in a log to assess the degree to which anger was successfully managed (Feindler & Ecton, 1986).

Poor Self-Concept

Black adolescents develop their self-concept and self-esteem from the reflected appraisals of parents, relatives, and peers in their own ethnic communities. Recently, in nonclinical samples, Black youth have consistently reported more positive self-concepts (Gibbs, 2003). This, however, is not the case among Black adolescents being referred for behavioral or psychological problems (Gibbs, 2003).

Adolescents with such problems may develop negative feelings about themselves because of their physical appearance, their atypical family structures, their lack of competence in culturally valued skills, or their feelings of racial victimization. In assessing this variable, clinicians should be aware of the significant sources of esteem for these youth, parental and peer reinforcement, and environmental factors. Some studies have indicated that athletic ability, verbal skills (e.g., rapping), and assertiveness may be the foundation of their self-concept (Gibbs, 2003).

Academic achievement is valued in some settings, whereas in other settings it is degraded. High achieving students in predominantly Black high schools, especially males, are sometimes ridiculed and accused of "acting White" (Gibbs,

H.Y.P.E.
(Healing Young People through Empowerment)

2003). This is likely exacerbated by the contemporary media's distortion of Black masculinity, which has become the internalized self-image for many Black adolescent boys. Some of these roles include "the absent father," "a pimp," "player," "athlete," and "underachiever" (Caldwell & White, 2001).

Mentorship

By the time most Black boys are between the ages of 10 and 13, they have observed "the doors of opportunity slam shut on the dreams" of many Black men in their lives (King, 1997). Conditions such as longer periods of unemployment, high incarceration rates, and poverty all disproportionately affect Black men in this country. Witnessing such conditions, often in overwhelming numbers, negatively impacts many Black adolescent boys' outlook on the future. In addition, many "at-risk" youth live in single, female-headed households in lower income areas, further limiting the opportunity for this group to find a successful male role model (King, 1997). Thus, for many Black adolescent boys, the involvement of a positive mentor whom they can identify with becomes a crucial part of their successful development into manhood.

During the past decade, mentoring programs for youth have become increasingly popular and widespread. The protective influence attached to mentoring relationships makes them ideal for youth who are considered "at-risk" by virtue of individual and/or environmental circumstances. Dubois et al. (2002) conducted a meta-analysis using 55 evaluations examining the effects of mentorship programs on youth. The authors found that all mentoring programs offered some benefit to the average youth; however, those based in theory and/or best practices had better outcomes. These mentoring programs had a positive effect on the five types of outcomes examined, which included: emotional/psychological, problem/high-risk behavior, social competence, academic/educational, and career/employment.

Part 2: The H.Y.P.E. Curriculum

H.Y.P.E. Program Design

The following therapeutic curriculum, "Healing Young People thru Empowerment" (H.Y.P.E.), is a 12-session program designed for Black adolescent boys whose primary diagnoses include Disruptive Behavior Disorders (DBD). The principal goals of the program are to help the participants critically think about their history of disruptive behavior, help them constructively handle "strong emotions," enhance their racial identity development, encourage accountability, augment and enhance personal growth, and finally increase appropriate behavior. Because traditional therapeutic models were designed by White professionals for White middle-class clients, the predominant conceptualization of mental health concerns is a reflection of Western values and ideas. Thus, the aim of the H.Y.P.E. program is to enhance the body of culturally appropriate interventions for Black adolescents. As a means of encouraging healthy racial identity development as well as enhancing open communication within the group, HHT will be integrated with the RT, Nigrescence theory, aspects of cognitive-behavioral, psychodynamic, and client-centered theories, and ICPS.

The procedural aspects of each session are based on the RT and HHT models. The session themes were developed by reviewing literature that explores salient issues proven to impact Black Americans, particularly adolescent boys. Additionally, the topics and issues highlighted within each session are guided by the Nigrescence and previously mentioned theories. Finally, the overarching belief of H.Y.P.E. rests in the tenet of the ICPS theory that suggests individuals are more likely to act appropriately when they have more skills to draw from.

H.Y.P.E.
(Healing Young People through Empowerment)

Group Composition

Although group composition is left to the discretion of the facilitator, it is recommended that members consist of Black adolescent boys between the ages of 13 and 21. The number of group members may also vary; however, it is suggested that the group include between six and 10 youth. Participants may be referred to the program by virtually any source including school staff, faculty, or administrators; mental health professionals; those within correctional or forensic settings; family members; community agencies; neighbors; and religious leaders.

H.Y.P.E. Intake Procedures

Prior to admission into the group, potential participants and a guardian should complete an intake procedure that includes a brief explanation of H.Y.P.E., an interview to gather pertinent background information, and completion of a consent form (see the Facilitator's Guide). If an initial intake session is not feasible, facilitators can develop their own method of obtaining necessary forms and information. In addition, parents and potential H.Y.P.E. members should understand that many of the songs used will include some explicit language. Confidentiality issues should also be addressed during the intake, with parents and youth understanding when information will and will not be disclosed.

Parental Consent and Involvement

As outlined in the Facilitator's Guide, an eight-session psychoeducational parent support group would be an ideal component of the H.Y.P.E. program. Most parents could benefit from learning effective parenting/relational skills, understanding adolescence, and receiving support from other parents with similar experiences; thus a parent group is designed to run concurrently with the H.Y.P.E youth group.

A parent group is not required, but it is recommended. Although the addition of a parent group would be effective, such a group would require more resources and may not be feasible. In this case the inclusion of simulated parental participation may be beneficial. This may include giving family members, guardians, or support persons an outline of the material covered in the sessions (including the songs) or letters written by youth that highlight the material covered in group. Additionally, giving parents and guardians psychoeducational materials on adolescent development and parenting may be useful.

Group Leadership

It is recommended that the H.Y.P.E. youth group be led by two co-facilitators to offer greater group coverage and a division of responsibilities. Furthermore, potential facilitators should ideally be mental health professionals, have educational or experiential experience with adolescents, or be youth advocates. Preferably co-facilitators would consist of a man and a woman, increasing opportunities for modeling positive male/female interactions. Group facilitators can be of any race or ethnicity, and it is imperative that they have personal insight into their own racial identity. Additionally, regardless of race and ethnicity, facilitators must be comfortable and open to discussing racism and oppression. It is also important that facilitators recognize the stimulus value their race, age, gender, and educational level bring to the group as these factors are addressed in varying ways throughout the group.

H.Y.P.E.
(Healing Young People through Empowerment)

Adopting a positive facilitative approach that is both unconditional and nonjudgmental can foster open dialogue among the members, which is a crucial part of the H.Y.P.E. group experience. Commending youth for sharing their experiences and feelings is important because H.Y.P.E. will mark the first time many of them have talked openly about themselves. Although including all the session material may be difficult, it is imperative that facilitators follow all the procedures outlined in this H.Y.P.E. Session Procedures section.

Facilitators should have some knowledge and/or experience working with adolescents who have received DBD diagnoses. Facilitators should also be open to listening to rap music and using it in a group format, even if it is not their preferred genre of music. Furthermore, they should preview the songs included in the H.Y.P.E. curriculum prior to starting a group; this will ensure a comfort level with the music and a familiarization with the themes. It is generally more helpful to make this assessment by listening to the music rather than just reading the lyrics. Familiarity with the rich history of Black people in America and the issues that disproportionately impact this group today is also crucial as these subjects are addressed in all the sessions. Finally, an awareness of local, national, and world news is important because each will have relevance in most H.Y.P.E. sessions.

Group Sessions
The H.Y.P.E. curriculum consists of 12 sessions, each of which focuses on an identified theme applicable to Black adolescent boys with DBD diagnoses. The session titles are either titles of rap songs or lyrics from a rap song. It is

recommended that the group meet at least once per week and that each session lasts for 90 to 120 minutes. The day(s) and time(s) of the group meetings will likely depend upon the availability of the facilitators and participants as well as the setting.

H.Y.P.E. groups can be conducted in most any setting that offers the following:

- privacy
- ample space to conduct at least one and possibly two concurrent groups (if a parent/guardian group is included)
- room for members to sit in a circle
- electrical outlets for AV equipment.

The session procedures include reciting the program creed, check in, presentation and processing of songs, delivery of psychoeducational material and corresponding activity, and an explanation of the weekly journal topic (homework). Many of the group activities will have an accompanying handout, giving facilitators the option of having members write and/or respond orally to the material. Additionally, some H.Y.P.E. songs have a "Rap Fact" listed, which should be shared with the group as a way to facilitate knowledge about rap history.

The Facilitator's Guide (Part 3) contains explanations of handouts for each session, process questions, and preparatory session material that should be reviewed before a H.Y.P.E. group is established. Prior to the first day of group, it is recommended that facilitators obtain the handouts shown in the Participant's Toolkit (Part 4) from www.letsgethype.com. Session song lyrics can also be found at www.letsgethype.com and

H.Y.P.E.
(Healing Young People through Empowerment)

www.ohhla.com. These forms can be stapled together to form the workbook. Even if workbooks are not created, the handouts provided in the Participant's Toolkit will be used during each session by group members and the facilitator(s).

H.Y.P.E. Session Procedures

Program Overview
The following provides an overview of the entire H.Y.P.E. curriculum.

SESSION 1
Topic: You Don't Know My Struggle
Theme: History of rap music, H.Y.P.E., and Disruptive Behavior Disorders
Purpose: Build cohesion within the group while establishing ground rules and exploring the disruptive behaviors members have engaged in.
Session Length: 120 minutes
Materials Needed: Songs, handouts, music, and a music player
Handouts Needed (see Participant's Toolkit): "I'm Not a Biter, I'm a Writer," "Brief History of Hip-Hop Culture," "Disruptive Behavior Checklist (from the DSM-IV-TR)," and "Journal Topic 1"
Procedures: Icebreaker – Overview – Ground Rules – Activity – Songs – Processing – Check Out

SESSION 2
Topic: Buck the World (Part 1)
Theme: Defining anger and exploring depression – real talk

Purpose: Group members will begin to identify past behavior in the context of the Social Cognitive Model, with a focus on their environment and personal factors. They will also begin to explore other emotions associated with anger, including sadness and depression, and the role oppression plays in these feelings.

Session Length: 120 minutes

Materials Needed: Songs, handouts, music, and a music player

Handouts Needed (see Participant's Toolkit): "What is Anger? What is Depression? What is Sadness" and "Journal Topic 2"

Procedures: Creed – Check In – Activity – Lesson – Songs – Processing – Check Out

SESSION 3

Topic: Buck the World (Part 2)

Theme: Developing an arsenal to constructively respond to strong emotions

Purpose: Group members will further examine the impact past and present experiences have had on their behavior. They will also begin to think about how other people have overcome negative personal and environmental obstacles.

Session Length: 120 minutes

Materials Needed: Songs, handouts, music, and a music player

Handouts Needed (see Participant's Toolkit): "What is Atonement," "Group Activity," and "Journal Topic 3"

Procedures: Creed – Check In – Activity – Songs – Processing – Check Out

H.Y.P.E.
(Healing Young People through Empowerment)
SESSION 4
(Adult Group Included)

Topic: I'm Black

Theme: Present day empowerment through exploration of the past

Purpose: Group members will discuss the ways Black leaders, and their own family members, have improved the opportunities available to Americans of color. The group will also explore what it means to be Black by sharing their own experiences.

Session Length: 120 minutes

Materials Needed: Songs, handouts, music, a music player, a computer, AV equipment, and a PowerPoint presentation

Handouts Needed (see Participant's Toolkit): "Pick a Family Member," "Lifetime Chances of Going to State or Federal Prison for the First Time," "Notable Black Leaders of Today a the Past," and "Journal Topic 4"

Procedures: Creed – Check In – Activity – Slideshow – Songs – Processing – Lesson – Check Out

SESSION 5

Topic: If My Homies Call

Theme: Let's talk about friends, enemies, and peer pressure

Purpose: Members will share the pressures they experience with peers, qualities a friend should embody, and a plan of action to use when confronted with negative peer pressure.

Session Length: 120 minutes

Materials Needed: Songs, handouts, music, and a music player

Handouts Needed (see Participant's Toolkit): "A Good Friend" and "Journal Topic 5"

Procedures: Creed – Check In – Activity – Songs – Processing
– Check Out

SESSION 6

Topic: I Really Miss My Homies

Theme: Death is a part of life…but it still hurts

Purpose: Members will share their experiences with death
and loss while learning various grief/loss models. Additionally,
the group will explore oppression by comparing causes of
death among Black and White Americans.

Session Length: 120 minutes

Materials Needed: Songs, handouts, music, and a music
player

Handouts Needed (see Participant's Toolkit): "Grief Models
and Activity," "Leading Causes of Death," and "Journal Topic
6"

Procedures: Creed – Check In – Songs – Processing – Lesson
– Activity – Check Out

SESSION 7

Topic: Dear Mama (Part 1)

Theme: Exploring my family's past in an effort to improve
my family's future

Purpose: Group members will share painful and pleasant
family memories and traditions while focusing on the feelings
evoked by each. Before the end of this session, participants
will identify a family member they want to have an improved
relationship with (to be further explored in Session 8).

Session Length: 120 minutes

Materials Needed: Songs, handouts, music, and a music
player

H.Y.P.E.
(Healing Young People through Empowerment)

Handouts Needed (see Participant's Toolkit): "Family Traditions and Memories" and "Journal Topic 7"
Procedures: Creed – Check In – Lesson – Songs – Processing – Activity – Check Out

SESSION 8
(Adult Group Included)

Topic: Dear Mama (Part 2)
Theme: Moving our families in a positive direction, one step at a time
Purpose: Group members will develop a plan of action designed to improve an aspect of their family that has caused them some distress in the past. They will also continue to explore the impact of oppression on their family.
Session Length: 120 minutes
Materials Needed: Songs, handouts, music, and a music player
Handouts Needed (see Participant's Toolkit): "My Family…" and "Journal Topic 8"
Procedures: Creed – Check In – Lesson – Songs – Processing – Check Out

SESSION 9

Topic: Git Up, Git Out, and Git Somethin (Part 1)
Theme: Lavish living later is the result of planning and hustling hard today
Purpose: Group members will begin to explore the impact of legal and illegal hustles on their futures. Participants will also participate in an adulthood simulation activity.
Session Length: 120 minutes
Materials Needed: Songs, handouts, music, and a music player

Handouts Needed (see Participant's Toolkit): "Consequences," "Snapshot of Adult Life," "Vignette A & B," "H.Y.P.E. Monthly Budget," and "Journal Topic 9"
Procedures: Creed – Check In – Lesson – Songs – Processing – Activity – Check Out

SESSION 10

Topic: Git Up, Git Out, and Git Somethin (Part 2)
Theme: Learning from those who have walked down this path before us
Purpose: Group members will begin to think about their dream life and ways they can make it happen. This can occur through discussion of the previous session's activity and/or exploring the lives of African-Americans (preferably men) who made mistakes as youth and went on to become successful.
Session Length: 120 minutes
Materials Needed: Songs, handouts, music, a music player, guest speakers (optional), and autobiographical and biographical media/books (optional)
Handouts Needed (see Participant's Toolkit): "My Dream Life" and "Journal Topic 10"
Procedures: Creed – Check In – Activity – Songs – Processing – Lesson – Check Out

SESSION 11

Topic: We've Got to Plan, Plot, Strategize
Theme: Using the lessons I've learned to guide my future
Purpose: Members will formulate short-term and long-term goals. They will begin to identify organizations that may offer

H.Y.P.E.
(Healing Young People through Empowerment)

mentoring or other opportunities to assist them in accomplishing their goals.

Session Length: 120 minutes

Materials Needed: Songs, handouts, music, a music player, and a mentor list (optional)

Handouts Needed (see Participant's Toolkit): "Goals" and "Journal Topic 11"

Procedures: Creed – Check In – Songs – Processing – Activity – Check Out

SESSION 12
(Adult Group Included)

Topic: I Remember

Theme: Celebrating the progress we've made as we continue to progress

Purpose: The goal of this session is to celebrate the progress the youth have made. Facilitators will encourage them to continue making improvements in their lives.

Session Length: 120 minutes

Materials Needed: Songs, handouts, music, a music player, and program certificates

Handouts Needed (see Participant's Toolkit): "Goals Wrap Up"

Procedures: Creed – Check In – Activity – Songs – Awards – Check Out

Session 1: You Don't Know My Struggle
Theme: History of rap music, H.Y.P.E., and Disruptive Behavior Disorders

The initial session provides members an opportunity to get to know one another and gain an understanding of the program in which they have agreed to participate. Developing ground rules and expectations are also tasks of this session. Finally, without naming their diagnoses, participants will use the Disruptive Behavior Checklist to describe their problematic behaviors and some of the negative consequences they have experienced.

Objectives

1. Get acquainted and begin to build group cohesion.
2. Gain an understanding of the H.Y.P.E. program.
3. Youth will look at their behaviors as actions they commit, as opposed to viewing them as statements of who they are.

Activities

1. Group members will engage in two icebreakers.
2. Facilitators will provide an overview of the program, which will include a brief history of hip-hop culture and rap music specifically.
3. Group members will establish ground rules.
4. Group members will identify two behaviors (e.g., stealing, truancy) they have engaged in that led to their involvement in this program.

Session Structure

1. Icebreakers

Name That Rapper. Group members will sit in a circle. Serving as "DJ," one facilitator will play a portion of a rap song for which the participants will attempt to guess the artist. No more than ten songs should be chosen for this icebreaker.

H.Y.P.E.
(Healing Young People through Empowerment)

Facilitators may also divide the group into two competing teams to encourage peer interactions and increase group cohesion.

I'm Not a Biter, I'm a Writer. Divide participants into two groups, and give them the following instructions: *"You and your group have 15 minutes to create a rap about 'unity'. After your time is up, your group will perform your song. There is only one requirement for song development and the group performance; you and your team members should make decisions about the song together."* An optional beat either spontaneously produced by team members or provided by facilitators who have access to instrumental pre-recorded songs, can be used.

2. **Overview of the Program**

- Give an overview of the H.Y.P.E. program, including a history of hip-hop culture and rap music, structure of the sessions, theories included in the H.Y.P.E. model, and expectations. A brief description of the H.Y.P.E. creator and the history of the program should also be provided.

- The facilitator(s) should explain, and then demonstrate the call and response format of the H.Y.P.E. creed. Next, the fact that members should say the name of a person they admire on the "Say influential person's name" portion of the creed, as opposed to repeating the name given by the person leading the creed should be explicitly explained. The facilitator(s) must also explain that each member will lead the creed at least once during the course of the group.

- Each H.Y.P.E. member should be provided with a work-book, that includes the handouts featured in the Participant's Toolkit and available at www.letsgethype.com, and H.Y.P.E. session song lyrics found on the H.Y.P.E. website and www.ohhla.com. The facilitator(s) should explain that the workbook will be used during every session, and great care should be taken with it."

- H.Y.P.E. group members should also be given a journal, created by stapling the 11 journal pages shown in the Participant's Toolkit and available at www.letsgethype.com. Journal entries can be written in poem, rap, or paragraph form, and it may be advantageous to indicate a minimum entry length not to exceed the space provided on the page. Journals should be reviewed regularly by the group facilitators, and guidelines for this should be shared during the first session."

3. **Ground Rules**

Ground rules are an effective tool for establishing expectations and addressing boundaries throughout the course of the program. Ground rules should be created collaboratively by group members and facilitators. Potential topics to be addressed include confidentiality, procedure for parent/guardian feedback (if applicable), expectations for participation, appropriate behavior and attitudes, and any other issues the group or facilitator(s) feel are important. To increase group participation, the facilitators may pass around a real or fictitious microphone (mic); only the group member holding the mic is allowed to speak. The mic should be passed to

H.Y.P.E.
(Healing Young People through Empowerment)

each person in succession so everyone is given a chance to contribute.

During this time, facilitators should also explicitly state their policy when members express thoughts of harming themselves or others. These ground rules should be recorded and referred to in future sessions as necessary.

4. **Activity**

Following the development of the ground rules, have the group think about behaviors they've engaged in that have led to negative consequences. This is done to smoothly transition the group into a discussion about disruptive behavior.

Next, direct the group to look at the *Disruptive Behavior Checklist (from the DSM-IV-TR)*" handout. Discuss and explain each behavior on the checklist. This should spark dialogue among the youth.

Additionally, the group members should identify behaviors they have engaged in.

5. **Presentation of Songs**

Present the following songs, and encourage participants to continue to openly share their experiences as they relate to the behaviors on the checklist. Given that many of these youth have likely taken little or no accountability for their actions, owning some of the disruptive behavior they have engaged in will help them identify personal problem areas.

Artist: Lil Boosie
Album: *Bad Azz 2 Mixtape* (2007)
Song: "You Don't Know My Struggle"
Rap Fact: Lil Boosie is from Baton Rouge, Louisiana.

Artist: Lil' Wayne
Album: *Tha Block is Hot* (1999)
Song: "F_ _k the World"
Rap Fact: *Tha Block is Hot* is Lil' Wayne's first solo album.

Artist: T.I.
Album: *I'm Serious* (2001)
Song: "Still Ain't Forgave Myself"
Rap Fact: *I'm Serious* is T.I.'s first album.

After each song is presented, group members will process questions and share feelings and thoughts evoked by the songs. They should also share at least one behavior that has led to negative consequences. Encourage group members to dialogue with each other.

6. Check Out

It may be necessary to give members an opportunity to check out at the conclusion of the session. This can be done in a variety of ways. For example, have each member say one word that summarizes how he is feeling. Or members can highlight specific disruptive behaviors they would like to explore, improve upon, or change over the next week.

Session 2: Buck the World (Part 1)

Theme: Defining anger and exploring depression – real talk

The goal of this session is to help group members understand their past and present behavior and the influences on their behavior. Initially group members are asked to define the words "anger," "sadness," and "depression." The Social Cognitive Model of Anger will be explained, and group

H.Y.P.E.
(Healing Young People through Empowerment)

members will be encouraged to think about ways oppression has impacted their feelings and behavior. By examining music that explores anger, hopelessness, suicide, and depression, group members are encouraged to openly share their experiences with "strong emotions." Finally, participants will begin to identify specific ways their environmental and personal factors have impacted their behavior.

Objectives

1. Group members will begin to learn and understand the elements of the Social Cognitive Model.
2. Group members will begin to identify triggers related to oppression that have led to negative behaviors and consequences.
3. Group members will begin to understand that a person's behavior is impacted by environment and personal factors.

Activities

1. Group members will name at least two feelings or emotions they've experienced that have led to significant distress/consequences in their lives.
2. Group members will share a personal or environmental factor that has influenced their behavior.
3. Group members will identify a socio-political issue, such as racial profiling by the police or store employees that may lead to strong emotions.

Session Structure
1. Recitation of the Group Creed and Check In

2. Activity (see the Facilitator's Guide)

The H.Y.P.E. Curriculum

The group will be asked to give their definitions of anger, sadness, and depression, and then the facilitator will define each term, which may foster some discussion. The facilitator will then present the lesson described below, after which group members should identify oppressive situations that caused them to feel strong emotions.

3. **Lesson: Overview of the Social Cognitive Model of Anger** (see the Pajares (2002) reference in the Facilitator's Guide)

Facilitators will provide group participants with an overview of the Social Cognitive Model of Anger. This model is based on the rationale that an individual's emotions and subsequent actions are regulated by personal and environmental factors. It is assumed that aggressive youth lack the necessary psychological resources for coping with problems and are, therefore, prone to reacting in an aggressive fashion when encountering a provocative situation. Thus, the cognitive-behavioral model is a skills-deficit one. In order to cope with stressors, the adolescent needs to develop these necessary skills.

One focus of this model is to help members better understand the factors that influence the thoughts and feelings that ultimately impact their behaviors. By recognizing how varying factors, including mood, experiences with oppression, and immediate environment influence their thoughts, youth should begin to recognize that their *interpretation* of situations influences their perceived behavioral options. Thus they will be better equipped to consider various alternatives to encountered situations, ultimately making better decisions.

H.Y.P.E.
(Healing Young People through Empowerment)

4. Presentation of Songs

Present the following songs, and encourage participants to openly share some of the behaviors or actions that have led to negative consequences. Given that many of the youth have likely not considered the impact of environmental and personal factors on their behavior, focusing on this will prove beneficial.

Artist: Nas
Album: *The Lost Tapes* (Sept. 2002)
Song: "No Idea's Original"
Rap Fact: Nas grew up in the Queensbridge housing projects in New York.

Artist: DMX
Album: *Flesh Of My Flesh, Blood Of My Blood* (Dec. 1998)
Song: "Slippin'"
Rap Fact: DMX released his debut and sophomore albums in the same year.

Artist: 2Pac
Album: *Me Against the World* (1995)
Song: "Lord Knows"
Rap Fact: This song starts and ends the same way.

Artist: Immortal Technique
Album: *The 3rd World* (2008)
Song: "The 3rd World"
Rap Fact: Immortal Technique is Afro-Peruvian, and he grew up in Harlem, New York. He has never signed to a major record label.

After each song is presented, group members will process questions and share feelings and thoughts evoked by the songs. Encourage participants to dialogue with each other.

5. **Optional Check Out**

It may be necessary at the conclusion of the session to give members an opportunity to check out. One approach is to have each member identify a disruptive behavior from Session 1 that they feel is directly linked to the social cognitive model.

Session 3: Buck the World (Part 2)

Theme: Developing an arsenal to constructively respond to strong emotions

During this session, participants will continue to share their past experiences with strong emotions. They will recall how they applied skills learned in Session 2 to various situations they experienced during the past week. Unconditional positive regard should be given during these exchanges, and members should be commended on their insight and willingness to share.

Objectives

1. Group members will begin to recognize the control they have over their actions as well as the difficulty of this task.
2. Group members will examine the concept of atonement and how it relates to their lives.
3. Group members will continue to explore the triggers that lead to negative consequences and increase their skills at controlling them.

H.Y.P.E.
(Healing Young People through Empowerment)

Activities
1. Group members will identify, in discussion, at least one time within the previous week when they utilized skills or insight gained in Session 1.
2. Group members will identify, in discussion, at least one risk and/or difficulty that may accompany changes in their behavior.
3. Group members will begin to develop their own plan of action for controlling strong emotions that have led to negative consequences in the past.

Session Structure
1. Recitation of the Group Creed and Check In

2. Review of Lesson
Facilitators should review the Social Cognitive Model of Anger that was introduced during the previous session. If there are members present who did not attend Session 2, ask those that were present to share the information. Facilitators should provide information that was omitted and answer any questions.

3. Group Activity (see the Facilitator's Guide)
Have a group member read Vignette 1 and then pose process questions to the group. Encourage members to dialogue with each other about the character's actions. The vignette's conclusion should then be shared with the group and also discussed.

Repeat these procedures for Vignette 2.
4. Presentation of Songs
Present the following songs, and encourage participants to openly share some of the behaviors or actions that have led to negative consequences.

Artist: Sheek Louch
Album: *After Taxes* (2005)
Song: "Pressure"
Rap Fact: Sheek Louch, Jadakiss, and Styles P made up the group The Lox.

Artist: Saigon f/ Trey Songz
Album: *The Greatest Story Never Told* (2006)
Song: "Pain in My Life"
Rap Fact: Saigon was sent to prison at 16 years old. He served seven years.

Artist: Lil Boosie
Song: "I Quit It"
Rap Fact: After the death of his father, Lil Boosie disclosed that he had diabetes.

After each song is presented, group members will process questions and share feelings and thoughts evoked by the songs. Encourage group members to dialogue with each other.

5. Optional Check Out

It may be necessary at the conclusion of the session, to give members an opportunity to check out. This can be done in a variety of ways. One example would be to have members identify the song they "felt" or could relate to the most.

Session 4: I'm Black
(Adult Group Included)

Theme: Present day empowerment through exploration of the past

H.Y.P.E.
(Healing Young People through Empowerment)

Group members will begin to explore the sacrifices made by members of their own families as well as prominent Black leaders within history, that have improved life for people of color in the 21st century. H.Y.P.E. members will also discuss what it means to be Black, including the positive and negative implications of their race. Racism and stereotypes will be defined. Group members will discuss the connection between the abolishment of slavery and the beginning of the American prison system. The lifetime chances of diverse populations going to prison should be explored and discussed. Finally, group members will be encouraged to consider their own legacy as Black Americans.

If parents/guardians attend this session, members will dialogue with them to foster intergenerational communication.

Objectives
1. Group members will begin to understand the sacrifices that have been made by family members as well as state and national leaders.
2. Group members will recognize the value in communicating with someone from another generation about their life experiences.
3. Group members will discuss the role they play in the legacy of Black America.

Activities
1. Group members will identify, in discussion, at least one person in their family who sacrificed or made a decision to improve the lives of their descendents.

2. Group members will identify, in discussion, at least two sources of negative images of Black people.
3. Group members will name the role they play in the legacy of Black America, identifying positive and negative attributes of their behavior, as well as their consequences.

Session Structure
1. Recitation of the Group Creed and Check In

2. Slide Show

A PowerPoint slideshow comprising painful and inspirational images of Black Americans will be shown with the song "I Can" by Nas playing in the background. A slideshow developed for this session by the author is available on www.letsgethype.com and includes the following events/ images:

- The Emmett Till funeral
- Lynchings
- Black socialites of 1920's Harlem
- Black soldiers who fought in World War II
- A picture of rappers from today and the past
- "Trees" (whelps) on the backs of former slaves
- President Barack Obama
- Michael Jackson
- Black athletes raising "Black Power" fists on the Olympic podium
- For facilitators who decide to develop their own, slideshows should last for the entire song. If slides are shown for four seconds each, the presentation will be comprised of approximately 48 slides.

H.Y.P.E.
(Healing Young People through Empowerment)

3. **Activities**

Have group members identify a family member whose sacrifices have improved their lives. Additionally, members should identify two places or situations in which they have seen Black people being portrayed negatively.

4. **Presentation of Songs**

Present the following songs to encourage participants to openly share their experiences with race and racism.

Artist: Ice Cube
Album: *Raw Footage* (2008)
Song: "Stand Tall"
Rap Fact: Ice Cube was a member of the pioneering group N.W.A. He wrote most of the group's songs.

Artist: Nas
Album: *Untitled* (2008)
Song: "N.I.*.*.E.R. "
Rap Fact: Nas' CD was originally slated to be titled *N.I.G.G.E.R.*

Artist: Graph
Song: "Heart of a Panther" (2007)
Rap Fact: This song is about Sean Bell, an innocent Black man who was killed by NYPD officers on his wedding day.
Slideshow Song

Artist: Nas
Album: *God's Son* (Dec. 2002)
Song: "I Can"

After each song is presented, group members will process questions and share feelings and thoughts evoked by the songs. Encourage group members to dialogue with each other.

5. **Freestyle with the Family**

Activity if family members are present: Each youth's family will break into dyads for approximately 25–35 minutes, and the adult will share a family story that showcases strength in the face of injustice or virtues such as bravery or honesty. Allow time for members to dialogue with their guardian/parent and ask any questions that will help them better understand their relative(s).

Following this activity, have the dyads come back together as a large group, and allow all members to share their reactions to the activity. Group members and their parents/guardians may also summarize the family stories they shared while in their dyads. Following this activity, the group should briefly review the list of notable African-Americans.

Activity if family members are not present: If family members are not included in the H.Y.P.E. group, more time can be taken to discuss songs. Additionally, the facilitators should review the chart labeled "Lifetime Chances of Going to State or Federal Prison for the First Time" with the group. Have members discuss some hypotheses explaining the differences and implications.

6. **Check Out**

At the conclusion of this session, have members discuss their responsibility and contribution to the legacy of Black America. This can be done by going around the group and allowing members to share their thoughts. It may be useful to allow the group members to write their responses prior to sharing them. Group members' attention should also be directed towards the chart labeled "Notable Black Leaders of Today and the Past" for their review outside of group. This is not homework, but it is encouraged.

Session 5: If My Homies Call

Theme: Let's talk about friends, enemies, and peer pressure

During this session, group members will talk about the qualities of a "good friend," and they will consider how their friends measure up to the identified qualities. The facilitator will challenge members to think about their experiences with peer pressure, how they respond to it, and the cost of not fitting in. Group members should identify and share possible plans of action they will use when confronted with negative peer pressure (based on their own experiences). Finally, participants should identify positive and negative encounters with friends as well as reasons why friends are necessary.

Objectives

1. Group members will begin to evaluate their peer group in comparison to the qualities they said a good friend should have.
2. Group members will become more skilled at thinking situations through before acting.
3. Group members will be better equipped to handle peer pressure.

The H.Y.P.E. Curriculum

Activities

1. Group members will develop a list of at least three characteristics they believe a good friend should embody.
2. Group members will share one experience with peer pressure.
3. Group members will share a positive and negative peer experience.

Session Structure

1. Recitation of the Group Creed and Check In

2. Activities: A True Friend (see the Facilitator's Guide)

Activity 1: Group members will be given three minutes to write three characteristics a good friend should have. The group will then share how their friends compare to their list.

Activity 2: Group members will either break into two or three groups or remain in a large group to discuss examples of peer pressure they've experienced and how they dealt with it.

3. Presentation of Songs

Present the following songs to encourage participants to openly share some of their experiences with friends and enemies.

Artist: 2Pac
Album: *2Pacalypse Now* (1992)
Song: "If My Homie Calls"
Rap Fact: *2Pacalypse Now* was 2Pac's first solo CD.

Artist: Jay-Z f/ John Legend
Album: *Kingdom Come* (2006)
Song: "Do U Wanna Ride" (Verse 1 & 2)
Rap Fact: *Kingdom Come* was Jay-Z's comeback CD following *The Black Album* and his retirement.

H.Y.P.E.
(Healing Young People through Empowerment)

Artist: Kanye West f/GLC and Paul Wall
Album: *Late Registration* (2005)
Song: "Drive Slow" (Verses 1 & 2)
Rap Fact: *Late Registration* was Kanye West's sophomore CD.

Artist: 2Pac
Album: *Better Dayz* (Disc 2, Nov. 2002)
Song: "Better Dayz"
Rap Fact: *Better Dayz* is a posthumously released two disc CD.

Artist: Nas
Album: *Illmatic* (1994)
Song: "1 Love"
Rap Fact: *Illmatic* was Nas' debut CD.

After each song is presented, group members will process questions and share feelings and thoughts evoked by the songs. Group members should be encouraged to dialogue with each other.

4. Optional Check Out

It may be necessary at the conclusion of the session to give members an opportunity to check out. This can be done by having members share one word that characterizes one of their friends.

Session 6: I Really Miss My Homies

Theme: Death is a part of life...but it still hurts

Group members will explore their experiences with death and loss. Initially, through examining the session songs, participants will share the circumstances involved in their loss, how they discovered the death/loss had occurred, the different emotions they experienced, and some of the thoughts they recall having. The group will be encouraged to discuss similarities between their various experiences with death/loss, including the causes and their reactions to them. Two models of grief and loss will be presented to the group, and members should relate their experience to the models. Finally, the group will examine the most common causes of death among Black and White Americans and develop hypotheses to explain the differences.

Objectives

1. Group members will understand the grieving process, thus normalizing their experiences with death.
2. Group members will feel more comfortable talking about their experiences with death/loss, and this will encourage them to use communication to work through difficult situations more productively.
3. Group members will begin to understand how oppression overwhelmingly impacts loss and death in the Black community.

Activities

1. Group members will share at least one experience with death/loss, specifically highlighting the feeling they experienced and how they coped.
2. Members will use one of the two grief/loss models to describe their experiences with loss.
3. Group members will develop and share one hypothesis that seeks to explain the different causes of death among African-Americans and Caucasian Americans.

H.Y.P.E.
(Healing Young People through Empowerment)

Session Structure

1. **Recitation of the Group Creed and Check In**

2. **Presentation of Songs**

Present the following songs, and encourage the participants to openly share their experiences and responses to grief and loss.

Artist: Lil Wayne f/ Nikki
Album: *The Carter II* (2005)
Song: "Get Over"
Rap Fact: *The Carter II* is the second part of *The Carter* album series.

Artist: Nas f/ Quan
Album: *Street's Disciple* (2004)
Song: "Just a Moment"
Rap Fact: *Street's Disciple* was Nas' first double CD.

Artist: T.I. f/ Jamie Foxx
Album: *King* (2006)
Song: "Live in the Sky"
Rap Fact: Philant Johnson, T.I.'s friend and personal assistant, was killed when they left a club in Cincinnati in 2006. This occurred shortly after *King* was released.

Artist: Mike Jones
Album: *Who is Mike Jones?* (2005)
Song: "Grandma"
Rap Fact: *Who is Mike Jones?* was Mike Jones' debut major label CD.

The H.Y.P.E. Curriculum

Artist: Notorious B.I.G.
Album: *Life After Death* (1997)
Song: "Miss U"
Rap Fact: Notorious B.I.G. was murdered in L.A. six months after 2Pac's death.

Artist: Lil' Wayne f/Robin Thicke
Album: Tha Carter III (2008)
Song: "Tie My Hands"
Rap Fact: More than one million copies of *Tha Carter III* were sold in the first week of its release.

After each song is presented, group members will process questions and share feelings and thoughts evoked by the songs. Encourage group members to dialogue with each other.

3. **Grief, Loss, and Causes of Death** (see the Facilitator's Guide)

Grief. Explain the Kubler-Ross Stages of Grief model, and allow participants to share their experiences with the various stages.

Loss. Depending on the experiences of the individual members, it may be advantageous to devote time to exploring loss and how similar it can feel to a loved one dying. Some time should be devoted to talking about the impact the disparity in drug sentencing has on Black Americans. Stages of loss as described by Dr. Roberta Temes in Living with an Empty Chair should be used when discussing this topic. Loss may include abandonment, incarceration, divorce, natural disaster, etc.

Causes of Death Activity. The group should continue to explore racism and oppression by examining the chart labeled "10 Leading Causes of Death." This chart compares and contrasts the causes and rates of death among Black and White Americans. Members should also develop a hypothesis to explain the differences. Related factors may include slavery, criminal justice, socioeconomic status, and education.

4. Optional Check Out

Each member will say one word that either describes a person they lost or how they dealt with this loss.

Session 7: Dear Mama (Part 1)

Theme: Exploring my family's past in an effort to improve my family's future

Group members will identify positive and negative family memories and traditions, explaining the feelings evoked by each and the impact the events had on their lives. Participants should think of ways in which negative traditions/memories can be diminished and positive ones increased. A brief history of the impact of racial oppression on Black families should be provided. Before the end of the session, group members should select a family member (guardian, parent, grandparent, sibling, cousin, foster/adoptive family member, etc.) with whom they would like to have an improved relationship. Some general goals should also be identified.

Objectives

1. Group members will identify areas of strength and weakness in their families.

2. Group members will begin to recognize the role they play within their families and areas in which they may facilitate changes within their families.
3. Group members will explore the effect the abandonment of their father (and/or other significant family member) has had on their lives.

Activities

1. Group members will identify, in discussion, at least one positive and one negative memory or tradition within their families.
2. Group members will identify, in discussion, at least one family member with whom they would like to have an improved relationship.
3. Group members will identify three non-specific goals designed to improve the relationship with this family member.

Session Structure

1. **Recitation of the Group Creed and Check In**
2. **Our Family History Activity** (see the Facilitator's Guide)

Group members will identify a positive and negative family memory or tradition. Positive memories or traditions may include holidays, family reunions, parties, trips, etc. Negative memories or traditions may include incarceration, abandonment of children, drug addiction, abuse, violence, death, etc. It may be necessary for the facilitator to bring up examples of negative memories or traditions to assist with this task.

Following this activity, a brief explanation of the Moynihan Report and the four roots of the Black family (as he saw it) should be given. Throughout the session, the Moynihan Report should be referred to as group members

H.Y.P.E.
(Healing Young People through Empowerment)

discuss the role of single mothers in their families, father abandonment, and child rearing.

3. Presentation of Songs

Present the following songs, and encourage the participants to openly share some of their positive and negative family experiences.

Artist: 2Pac
Album: *Me Against the World* (1995)
Song: "Dear Mama"
Rap Fact: Tupac's mother was a member of the Black Panther Party. While she was pregnant with Tupac, she defended herself in a conspiracy trial that included 156 counts. A month before he was born, she was acquitted of all charges.

Artist: Ed O.G. & Da Bulldogs
Album: *Life of a Kid in the Ghetto* (1991)
Song: "Be a Father to Your Child"
Rap Fact: Ed O.G. is also known as Edo G. and is from Roxbury, Massachusetts.

Artist: Little Brother f/ Darren Brockington
Album: *The Minstrel Show* (2005)
Song: "All for You"
Rap Fact: The group Little Brother met at North Carolina Central University in Durham, North Carolina.

Artist: Rick Ross f/ Rodney
Album: *Trilla* (2008)
Song: "I'm Only Human" (Chorus and Verse 1)
Rap Fact: Rick Ross is from Miami, Florida.

The H.Y.P.E. Curriculum

Artist: Lupe Fiasco f/ Gemini, Sarah Green
Album: *Food & Liquor* (2006)
Song: "He Say She Say"
Rap Fact: Lupe Fiasco is from one of the roughest areas of Chicago.

After each song is presented, group members will process questions and share feelings and thoughts evoked by the songs. Encourage group members to dialogue with each other.

4. **Improving Family Relationships Activity** (see the Facilitator's Guide)

After the session songs are processed, members will identify a family member with whom they wish to have an improved relationship. They will also identify three non-specific areas they would like to improve.

5. **Optional Check Out**

Group members will identify the person with whom they would like to have an improved relationship. They should only give the person's name or their relationship to them.

Session 8: Dear Mama (Part 2) (Adult Group Included)

Theme: Moving our families in a positive direction, one step at a time

Group members will continue to explore family inter-actions and relationships. If a formal parent group has formed, youth and guardians/parents will create a strategy, based on the three areas highlighted in Session 7, to improve their relationships. They will then come together, share their plans,

H.Y.P.E.
(Healing Young People through Empowerment)

and develop a poster board for the family, outlining areas identified for improvement. Families will share their goals with the large group.

For youth groups that don't have a formal parent/guardian group, most of the time will be spent exploring how various forms of oppression impact Black families. The role of intergenerational patterns will be discussed. Facilitators can share aspects of Douglas Blackmon's book, *Slavery by Another Name*, with group members.

Objectives

1. Group members will own the impact they have on their family's future traditions and interactions.
2. Group members will communicate the strengths and weaknesses they have seen within the family.
3. Group members will gain an even clearer understanding of the impact of oppression on Black families.

Activities

1. Group members will develop a strategy for improving their relationships with identified family members (if there is a formal parent group).
2. Each family will develop a poster that outlines the goals they identified in collaboration (if there is a formal parent group).
3. Youth and guardian members will continue to identify strengths and weaknesses within their families (if there is a formal parent group).
4. Group members will self-disclose a familial situation that was impacted by a form of oppression discussed in group.

5. Group members will identify actions they can take to positively impact their families.

Session Structure
1. Recitation of the Group Creed and Check In

2. Oppression and My Family Activity (see the Facilitator's Guide)

Group members should identify at least one way that oppression has impacted their families. The information shared from the Moynihan Report in "Dear Mama" (Part 1) should be reviewed again and utilized to assist members in the activity. If there is a formal guardian group, minimal time should be spent on this activity.

3. Presentation of Songs
Present the following songs, and encourage participants to openly talk about their families.

Artist: Scarface
Album: *The World is Yours* (1993)
Song: "Now I Feel Ya" (Verse 1)
Rap Fact: Scarface is from Houston, Texas, and was a member of the Geto Boys.

Artist: 2Pac
Album: *Greatest Hits* (1998)
Song: "Unconditional Love"
Rap Fact: Seven of 2Pac's posthumously released albums went platinum.

H.Y.P.E.
(Healing Young People through Empowerment)

Artist: Jay-Z
Album: *The Black Album* (Nov. 2003)
Song: "December 4th"
Rap Fact: *The Black Album* was originally slated to be Jay-Z's last recorded album. He made this decision after being appointed CEO of Def Jam Records.

Artist: Nas
Album: *The Lost Tapes* (Sept. 2002)
Song: "Poppa Was a Player"
Rap Fact: Nas' father, Olu Dara, is a jazz musician.

After each song is presented, group members will process questions and share feelings and thoughts evoked by the songs. Encourage group members to dialogue with each other.

4. **Interactive Activity with the Adult Group** (if a formal family group is used)

Youth and guardian member dyads will elaborate on the goals or areas of improvement they identified during Session 7. Next, the youth/guardian teams will share their ideas with the rest of the group so everyone can contribute thoughts and suggestions. Teams should then create a poster that may include goals, objectives, strategy details, and helpful techniques that were discussed during the session.

5. **Optional Check Out**

Each member should say one word that summarizes how he/she is feeling.

Session 9: Git Up, Git Out, and Git Somethin (Part 1)

The H.Y.P.E. Curriculum

Theme: Lavish living later is the result of planning and hard hustling today

Participants will identify long and short-term consequences of various illegal hustles, particularly those they have engaged in. Members will then identify the skills used when engaging in various illegal hustles as well as a comparable legal hustle that requires the same or similar skills. Finally, participants will complete and discuss the "Snapshot of Adult Life" exercise.

Objectives
1. Group members will begin to recognize that the life they lead now will impact their lives as adults.
2. Group members will become more cognizant of the long-term impact of positive and negative behavior, thus increasing their motivation to behave in a socially appropriate manner.
3. Group members will begin to identify future goals.

Activities
1. Group members will identify, in discussion, at least two long-term and short-term consequences of an illegal hustle.
2. Group members will identify skills used in illegal jobs that could be useful in a legitimate job.
3. Group members will complete the "Snapshot of Adult Life" activity and discuss it at the end of the session.

Session Structure
1. Recitation of the Group Creed and Check In

H.Y.P.E.
(Healing Young People through Empowerment)

2. **Activity**

Group members will identify and dialogue about positive and negative short- and long-term consequences of an illegal hustle. Positive consequences can include making money, earning respect, obtaining goods, being your own boss, making your own schedule, avoiding the hiring process, etc. Negative consequences may include being incarcerated, putting your family in harm's way, being killed, becoming addicted to the product or activity, missing out on family memories, etc.

3. **Presentation of Songs**

Present the following songs, and encourage participants to openly share their goals and dreams.

Artist: Jay-Z
Album: *The Black Album* (Nov. 2003)
Song: "Allure"
Rap Fact: Producer Pharrell Williams produced this song for Jay-Z.

Artist: Too $hort
Album: *Short Dog's In the House* (1990)
Song: "The Ghetto"
Rap Fact: Too $hort is from Oakland, California.

Artist: The Game f/Lil Wayne
Album: *L.A.X.* (2008)
Song: "My Life"
Rap Fact: After graduating from high school, The Game attended Washington State University on a basketball scholarship for one semester before being expelled.

The H.Y.P.E. Curriculum

Artist: Twista f/ Pharrell
Album: *The Day After* (Oct. 2005)
Song: "Lavish"
Rap Fact: Twista was honored in the 1992 Guinness Book of World Records as the world's fastest rapper.

After each song is presented, group members will process questions and share feelings and thoughts evoked by the songs. Encourage group members to dialogue with each other.

4. **Snapshot of Adult Life** (see the Facilitator's Guide)
All members will share the aspect(s) of the activity that surprised them the most, and why. Group members should share the most frustrating part of their mock adult lives, with those selecting the lowest level of educational attainment going first.

5. **Optional Check Out**
Group members will briefly share whether their views of adult life were similar or different from what they experienced during the activity.

Session 10: Git Up, Git Out, and Git Somethin (Part 2)

Theme: Learning from those who have walked down this path before us
The group will discuss the laws that perpetuate the disparity between crack cocaine and powder cocaine sentencing, its relevance to Black boys and men, and the overwhelming impact it has had on Black families.

H.Y.P.E.
(Healing Young People through Empowerment)

If the setting allows, people from the community will be invited to participate in one of two panel discussions with the group members. The first panel will include individuals who are currently dealing with the negative consequences created by poor choices they have made. The next panel will include individuals who are successful in their particular sectors as a result of dedication and hard work. Although the second panel may include individuals who have suffered consequences for negative actions in the past, they should have moved beyond them at this point in their lives.

If bringing in guest speakers is not feasible, group members instead will be given five minutes to fantasize about their "dream lives" as adults, including their future occupations, residences, family compositions, and other details they wish to envision. Next, they will be challenged to identify ways they can make these dreams a reality, including steps they can take now as teenagers (education, experience, and training requirements). For the remainder of the session, group members will identify resources that can help them realize their dreams.

Objectives
1. Group members will identify with the panel members' stories and feel more empowered to work towards their goals (if a panel was convened).
2. Group members will reevaluate some of the constraints they previously believed limited them.
3. Group members will recognize the necessity of having an education, skill, and/or a trade.

Activities
1. Group members will identify, in discussion, at least one community person they wish to network with over the next week (if a panel was convened).

2. Group members will describe their dream lives based on the information they gathered during this and previous sessions.
3. Group members will identify, in discussion, an academic major, occupation, trade, or skill necessary to fulfill their ultimate goals/dreams.

Session Structure
1. Recitation of the Group Creed and Check In

2. **Activity** (if a panel is not convened)

Group members will identify and share their dream lives and ways they can make their dream lives a reality. It is likely that at least one youth will have great difficulty with this task. If this happens, group members should be encouraged to think as "big" as they can. The facilitator should emphasize that no dream is too big or too far out of reach.

3. **Presentation of Songs**

Present the following songs, and encourage participants to think about their futures.

Artist: Young Jeezy f/ Keyshia Cole
Album: *The Inspiration* (2006)
Song: "Dreamin'"
Rap Fact: Young Jeezy was a volunteer for President Barack Obama's 2008 Presidential campaign.

Artist: OutKast f/ Goodie Mob
Album: *Southernplayalisticadillacmuzik* (1994)
Song: "Git Up, Git Out"
Rap Fact: In 2004, OutKast became the first rap group to win a Grammy for Album of the Year.

H.Y.P.E.
(Healing Young People through Empowerment)

Artist: T.I.
Album: *Urban Legend* (2004)
Song: "Prayin for Help"
Rap Fact: T.I. was nicknamed "Tip" after his great-grandfather.

Artist: Ludacris f/Common
Album: *Theater of the Mind* (2008)
Song: "Wake Up"
Rap Fact: DJ Chris Lova Lova was Ludacris' radio personality name. His position at the Atlanta radio station helped launch his rap career.

After each song is presented, group members will process questions and share feelings and thoughts evoked by the songs. Encourage group members to dialogue with each other.

4. **Community Member Panels** (If formal panels are convened for this session, each should last about 30 minutes.)
Panel 1: This panel will be comprised of individuals who are currently suffering the consequences of their negative actions. Facilitators may solicit such individuals through probation departments, organizations that assist felons, job training centers, churches, etc. Discussion topics may include the age when they began engaging in negative behaviors, educational attainment, actions/consequences suffered, their lives now, and how they are atoning.
Panel 2: This panel will be comprised of individuals who are currently successful in their various sectors as a result of hard work, planning, and determination. Facilitators should solicit such individuals through professional Black organizations, fraternities/sororities, universities, or the Better Business Bureau. Discussion topics may include the age when they

realized "this is what I want to do," educational attainment, sacrifices they made in reaching their goals, and their lives now. Alternative Exercise: If forming a panel is not appropriate for the session, biographies of famous, accomplished, or dysfunctional people can be shared for discussion.

5. Optional Check Out
Each group member will say one word that summarizes how he is feeling.

Session 11: We've Got to Plan, Plot, Strategize

Theme: Using the lessons I've learned to guide my future
The aim of this session is to further encourage group members to develop goals by participating in cooperative educational experiences. Group members will develop one-year and five-year goals, and they will identify the steps to achieve them. Facilitators should develop and distribute a mentor list to group members that may include sources listed on the "Mentor Program Possible Referral Sources" handout in the Facilitator's Guide (if referrals are feasible). If providing referrals is not an option, the facilitator should continue to challenge members to consider the fields for which their talents and skills (particularly those previously used for negative means) can best be utilized.

Objectives
1. Group members will begin to develop long-term goals and identify the skills necessary to achieve them.
2. Group members will be assigned cooperative learning experiences that will facilitate the achievement of their goals and dreams (if a formal referral program is used).

H.Y.P.E.
(Healing Young People through Empowerment)

3. Group members will become more empowered to make good choices so that they won't jeopardize their future goals.

Activities

1. Group members will develop two concrete, long-term goals and the steps they will take to fulfill them.
2. Group members will select three businesses or organizations from which they could gain practical experience; they will identify two skills they would hope to develop at each.
3. Group members will identify, in discussion, a specific behavior they will monitor and/or improve upon to ensure their goals and dreams are realized.

Session Structure
1. Recitation of the Group Creed and Check In

2. Presentation of Songs
Present the following songs, and encourage participants to think about their goals.

Artist: T.I.. f/ Justin Timberlake
Album: *Paper Trail* (2008)
Song: "Dead and Gone"
Rap Fact: T.I. is a Grammy award winning artist.

Artist: Mike Jones
Album: *Who is Mike Jones?* (2005)
Song: "5 Years From Now"
Rap Fact: Mike Jones is the owner of the Ice Age Entertainment label.

The H.Y.P.E. Curriculum

Artist: T.I. f/ Common and Pharrell
Album: *King* (2006)
Song: "Goodlife"
Rap Fact: Common's stage name when he entered the rap game was Common Sense.

Artist: Young Buck
Album: *Buck the World* (2006)
Song: "Slow Ya Roll"
Rap Fact: Young Buck is from Nashville, Tennessee. He got his first big break with former Cash Money Records rapper Juvenile and his group UTP.

After each song is presented, group members will process questions and share feelings and thoughts evoked by the songs. Encourage group members to dialogue with each other.

3. **Formulating a Plan** (if mentors are used)
Members will be given a mentor list that includes organization names, the activities they offer, and a description of the professions. Group members will select the organization they would like to be referred to. This selection will be based on the skills and experiences they will need to develop. Participants should be able to articulate the rationale for their selections. Facilitators should review the "Mentor Program Possible Referral Sources" in the Facilitator's Guide, for potential professional organizations.

When the selections have been made, the group will convene and individually share the experiences they selected, their rationales, as well as their plans for dealing with obstacles. The remaining members and facilitators will ask questions and offer suggestions about each individual's selections and explanations.

H.Y.P.E.
(Healing Young People through Empowerment)

Based on the selections and discussions, the facilitators will refer the members to an organization. This information will be shared with parents/guardians either in person after the session or through written correspondence.

4. **Activity** (see the Facilitator's Guide)

Group members will be asked to develop one-year and five-year goals and the steps needed to achieve those goals. Have group members share their goals with the group. If a formal referral program is not included, the facilitator should challenge members to research and contact businesses, organizations, and programs on their own as a practical way to realize their dreams.

5. **Optional Check Out**

Have group members identify one behavior or activity they should monitor, change, or avoid that will help them achieve their goals.

Session 12: I Remember

Theme: Celebrating the progress we've made as we continue to progress

The entire session will be dedicated to celebrating the accomplishments the youth have achieved over the course of the program. If a formal parent group was formed, adult members will be invited to attend. Participants will listen to the Session Songs and then break into family dyads. Within these dyads, each will identify changes they have seen in the other family member as well as the impact those changes have had on them. Members will then share specific things about themselves they are still willing to improve upon, and they will develop a strategy for maintaining the success they have achieved thus far.

If a formal parent group was not formed, the youth will identify the changes they have experienced during the program, their impact, and the areas that still need work. Finally, participants will receive certificates of appreciation and enjoy a party.

Objectives

1. Group members will feel pride in their completion of the H.Y.P.E. program.
2. Group members will celebrate each other's accomplishments, which will strengthen their bonds.
3. Group members will be inspired to continue working towards their goals and avoid disruptive, negative, and harmful behaviors.

Activities

1. Group members will fellowship together, listen to the Session Songs, and participate in a certificate of completion presentation ceremony.
2. Group members will identify three things they are willing to do outside of H.Y.P.E. to fulfill their goals and/or increase positive behavior.

Session Structure

1. **Recitation of the Group Creed and Check In**
2. **Activity** (see the Facilitator's Guide)

Group members will identify three things they can continue to do to accomplish their goals. Member responses should be shared with the group. It's likely that during this time, youth who initially had difficulty identifying goals in previous sessions will easily name goals and the steps they can take to make them happen.

H.Y.P.E.
(Healing Young People through Empowerment)

3. Presentation of Songs and Celebration with Food

Present the following songs, and encourage the participants to celebrate life, their families, and their achievements. At this time, members can be served the food brought in for the celebration.

Artist: Lil Boosie
Album: *Bad Azz* (2006)
Song: "I Remember"
Rap Fact: Boosie was signed by Trill Entertainment, which was backed by the late Pimp C of the group Underground Kings (better known as UGK).

Artist: 2Pac f/ Danny Boy
Album: *I Ain't Mad at Cha* (Video) (1996)*
Song: "I Ain't Mad at Cha"
Rap Fact: This video closely mirrored the events that took place when 2Pac was fatally shot.

Artist: Twista f/ Cee-Lo
Album: *Kamikaze* (2004)
Song: "Hope"
Rap Fact: Cee-Lo started his mainstream career in the group Goodie Mob. He later had a solo career and eventually developed Gnarles Barkley, an alternative duo.

Artist: Nas f/Lauryn Hill
Album: *It Was Written* (1996)
Song: "If I Ruled the World"
Rap Fact: Lauryn Hill's solo CD, *The Miseducation of Lauryn Hill*, earned a record 10 Grammy nominations.

After each song is presented, group members will process questions and share feelings and thoughts evoked by the songs. Encourage group members to dialogue with each other.

4. Awards and Recognition

If a formal parent group is included, following the dyad discussions, have adult and youth members come together in a large group. Each dyad will discuss the points of pride identified and a strategy for maintaining the change. Facilitators will offer encouraging and supportive words to the group. If a formal parent group was not included, facilitators should offer encouraging words and implore participants to stay focused on the future. They will then individually present group members with the H.Y.P.E. Certificate of Completion available at www.letsgethype.com.

5. Final Check Out

One at a time, each member will talk about the group's impact on his outlook on life. Next, have each group member write his name at the top of a piece of paper. Pass the paper around the circle so that all members can write a positive statement about the person listed at the top. Repeat the process until all members have received positive statements. Participants can refer to this paper whenever they are in need of encouragement.

H . Y . P . E .

Healing

Young

People

Thru

Empowerment

FACILTATOR'S GUIDE

H.Y.P.E.
(Healing Young People through Empowerment)
Technical Support

Please logon to www.letsgethype.com for program handouts, links to H.Y.P.E. songs, lyrics, the Session 4 Slideshow, technical assistance, the newest program updates, and other program material. Additionally, the latest hip-hop news and links to relevant new songs that can be played during "down times" (e.g. when members arrive before group begins) can be found at www.letsgethype.com. Dr. Adia McClellan Winfrey can also receive your questions and feedback through the H.Y.P.E. website.

Recommended Measure

In an effort to measure the effect of youth participation in H.Y.P.E., it is recommended that youth complete the Pre-Test/Post-Test on the following page during the intake or at the beginning of the first session, and again at the end of the final session. Because the same measure is used for the pre-test and post-test, it is imperative that the facilitator or youth circle the correct word to indicate which test it is.

On the "Aggression" scale of this measure, "false" endorsements suggest the individual uses non-aggressive methods to handle difficult situations. On the "Self-Efficacy" scale, "true" responses indicate confidence in one's ability to achieve academically. "False" endorsements on the "Future Aspirations" scale suggest an optimistic outlook on life. And "true" responses on the "Employment" scale are indicative of positive attitudes about work.

To measure H.Y.P.E. group members' behavioral and attitudinal changes before and after participation, the facilitator can compare the number of true and false responses on the pre- and post- test scales. Increased "false" endorsements on the post-test when compared to the pre-test, may indicate positive change on the "Aggression" and "Future Aspirations" scales. On the "Self-Efficacy" and "Employment" scales, increased "true" endorsements may suggest behavioral and attitudinal improvements in these areas.

PRE-TEST/POST-TEST (Circle one)

Please read each question carefully, and based on your true thoughts and feelings, check either "true" or "false".

Aggression

1) It makes you feel big and tough when you push someone around.
___ True   ___False

2) If you back down from a fight, everyone will think you are a coward.
___True   ___False

3) Sometimes you only have two choices when confronted by someone else; punch or get punched.
___True   ___False

Self-Efficacy

4) I will graduate from high school.
___True   ___False

5) I will learn a trade and/or graduate from college.
___True   ___False

6) I don't need to fight because there are other ways to deal with anger.
___True   ___False

7) I will get a job I really want.
___True   ___False

H.Y.P.E.
(Healing Young People through Empowerment)

Future Aspirations

8) I will probably die before I am 30 years old.

___True   ___False

9) I will probably never have enough money.

___True   ___False

10) Bad things happen to me, and people like me.

___True   ___False

11) I will have more bad times than good times when I grow up.

___True   ___False

12) Even if I work hard, I'll probably never get ahead.

___True   ___False

Employment

13) I am skilled enough to do a job well.

___True   ___False

14) I admire people who work hard, and make money legally.

___True   ___False

15) Working hard at a job will pay off in the end.

___True   ___False

Part 3: Facilitator's Guide

Consent Form for Participation in the H.Y.P.E. Program

I, _____ and my parent/guardian
_____, agree to voluntarily participate in the H.Y.P.E. Program. We understand that:

- o Hip-hop culture, and rap music specifically, are necessary components of the H.Y.P.E. program. The unedited versions of songs are utilized for this program, and many contain explicit lyrics.
- o The mission of the H.Y.P.E. Program is to offer culturally appropriate interventions to Black adolescent boys and their parents/guardians using a holistic approach that focuses on parent involvement, racial identity, cognitive interpersonal skills, self-concept, appropriate emotional expression and regulation, and mentorship.
- o The H.Y.P.E adolescent and adult groups may be facilitated by a variety of mental health professionals, including clinical psychologists, undergraduate and graduate students, social workers, family therapists, counselors, or youth advocates.
- o Pre- and post-group questionnaire packets may be administered to adolescent participants and may include measures that assess depression, anxiety, disruptive behavior, anger, self-concept, or racial identity. Parent/guardian participants will also be responsible for completing a pre- and post-group questionnaire in which they will rate different aspects of their adolescent's behavior.
- o Parent/guardian participants may be provided a H.Y.P.E. Session Procedures handout as well as the lyrics of songs played during each of the sessions. This will

93

H.Y.P.E.
(Healing Young People through Empowerment)

help to guide the parent sessions and encourage parents to discuss the weekly topics with their child at home.

o There are 12 sessions in the H.Y.P.E. Program. The duration of each session and total program is up to the discretion of the facilitator.

o All information will remain confidential, and identifiable information will be concealed from others outside of the group.

o If the facilitators suspect the presence of serious emotional or psychological distress, the parent/ guardian will be referred to individual psychotherapy (if the youth is not already engaged in therapy). If participants reveal suicidal or homicidal thoughts or actions, this may lead to further action.

We have read the above statements, asked the necessary questions, and expressed concerns. These questions and/or concerns have been answered. Our signatures below indicate that we hereby give informed and free consent to be voluntary participants in the H.Y.P.E. Program. I have been given a copy of this consent form.

_____

Signature of Adult Participant / Date

_____

Signature of Adolescent Participant / Date

_____

Signature of Co-Facilitator / Date

_____

Print name of Adolescent Participant / Date

Part 3: Facilitator's Guide

H.Y.P.E. Parent/Guardian Sessions (Optional)

H.Y.P.E. Parent/Guardian Group. The H.Y.P.E. parent/ guardian group is an optional eight group component of H.Y.P.E., which occurs during the same period as the H.Y.P.E. youth group. Three of the eight adult sessions are combined with the H.Y.P.E. youth sessions, while the remaining five groups are conducted exclusively with parent/guardian members. Much of the information covered in the adult group will mirror the youth group, although issues related to adolescent development and parenting will be included as well. Conducting a parent/guardian group will require additional preparation by the facilitator prior to starting the group; particularly in the area of youth development and parenting. While much of the information in Part 1 of this book can be integrated into the parent group, facilitators may also need to refer to the following reference:

> Cody, P.S. (2006) Working with oppositional youths using Brief Strategic Family Therapy. In Franklin, C, Harris, M.B., & Allen-Meares, P. (Eds.), *The school services sourcebook: A guide for school-based professionals* (pp. 671–680). New York: Oxford University Press.

In addition, facilitators of parent/guardian groups can go to www.letsgethype.com to receive technical support from the author and relevant handouts. The eight H.Y.P.E. sessions are outlined below:

Session 1 (Session should occur during the week of Youth session 1 or 2)
Objective: Parent/guardian members will gain a better understanding of the history of hip-hop culture, their child's

H.Y.P.E.
(Healing Young People through Empowerment)

disruptive behavior, and adolescent development. For the icebreaker, group members will complete the "I'm Not a Biter, I'm a Writer" exercise, creating raps about "parenthood." The facilitator should review the H.Y.P.E. creed with the parent group, as their sessions will also begin with it. Members will listen to the three songs from youth session 1, and the first two songs from youth session 2.

Session Length: 120 minutes

Materials Needed: music, lyrics, and a music player

Handouts Needed (see the Participant's Toolkit and **www.letsgethype.com**): "I'm Not a Biter, I'm a Writer," "Brief History of Hip-Hop Culture," "Disruptive Behavior Checklist (From DSM-IV-TR)," "What is Anger? What is Depression? What is Sadness," and "Adolescent Development"

Group Format: Icebreaker – Overview – Lesson – Songs – Processing – Check Out

Session 2: (Session should occur during the week of Youth session 2 or 3)

Objective: Group members will explore their expectations of their teenagers in relation to the adolescent development discussed in Session 1. Group members will also explore the following four parenting styles: authoritarian, authoritative, permissive, and uninvolved. For homework, adults will identify one or two family members who were influential in their family. They should also think about inspirational stories of influential Black Americans they have not previously shared with their teenager. This information will be utilized in the first combined session. Adult group members will listen to the last two youth session 2 songs and the three youth session 3 songs.

Part 3: Facilitator's Guide

Session Length: 120 minutes
Materials Needed: music, lyrics, and a music player
Handouts Needed (see www.letsgethype.com): "Parenting Styles"
Group Format: Creed – Lesson – Songs – Processing – Check Out

Session 3: Youth and Parents/Guardians (Combined for Youth session 4)
Objective: Adult members will share inspiring stories with their teenagers about famous and familial Black Americans who have positively influenced their lives. Adults will also share some of the negative experiences they've dealt with as a result of being a Black person in this society.
Session Length: 120 minutes
Materials Needed: Songs, handouts, music, a music player, a computer, AV equipment, and a PowerPoint presentation
Handouts Needed (see Participant's Toolkit): "Pick a Family Member," "Lifetime Chances of Going to State or Federal Prison for the First Time," "Notable Black Leaders of Today a the Past"
Procedures: Creed – Check In – Activity – Slideshow – Songs – Processing – Lesson – Check Out

Session 4: (Session should occur during the week of Youth session 5)
Objective: Group members will share some of the changes they have implemented in their families based on things learned in the group. They should also address some of the challenges they've experienced since implementing these changes. Facilitators will continue to remind parents of the

H.Y.P.E.
(Healing Young People through Empowerment)

developmental milestones typical for adolescence, and the four parenting styles. For homework, parents will be encouraged to talk to their teenagers about their friends. This will include learning about their friends' common interests, their ages, where they met, the amount of time they spend together, and their friends' goals. Process the five songs from Youth session 5, and three songs from Youth session 6.

Session Length: 120 minutes

Materials Needed: music, lyrics, and a music player

Handouts Needed (see Participant's Toolkit): "A Good Friend"

Group Format: Check In – Lesson – Processing – Songs – Processing – Check Out

Session 5: (Session should occur during Youth session 6)
Objective: Members will share the biggest surprise and greatest fear about their teenager's choices in friends. Parents should review the "Grief Models and Activity" handout, and name individuals who've died that their youth are likely to mention. It may also be beneficial for parent/guardian members to share their own reactions to losses likely to be mentioned by youth members. When relevant, adult group members will identify times when they have been estranged from their children, and its impact on them. Parents should also complete the "Family Traditions and Memories" handout during this session. For homework, parents will explore the parenting mistakes they have made and the consequences of those mistakes. Group members will listen to, and briefly process three youth session 6 songs and five youth session 7 songs.

Part 3: Facilitator's Guide

Session Length: 120 minutes
Materials Needed: music, lyrics, and a music player
Handouts Needed (see Participant's Toolkit): "Grief Models and Activity," "Leading Causes of Death," "Family Traditions and Memories"
Group Format: Check In – Lesson – Processing – Songs – Processing – Check Out

Session 6: Youth and Parents/Guardians (Combined for Youth Session 8)

Objective: Youth and adult group members will develop a plan of action designed to improve an aspect of their family that has caused them some distress in the past. They will also continue to explore the impact of oppression on their family.
Session Length: 120 minutes
Materials Needed: music, lyrics, a music player, poster board, and markers
Handouts Needed (see Participant's Toolkit): "My Family…"
Procedures: Creed – Check In – Lesson – Songs – Processing – Check Out

Session 7: (Session should occur during youth session 9 or 10)

Objective: Adult members will be given resources for helping their children fulfill their goals. They will also be challenged to set goals for themselves to improve their circumstances, which will ultimately benefit their children. Another important aim of this session is emphasizing the importance of consistency, and each member should be encouraged to share their experiences and difficulty with this. Songs from youth sessions 9, 10, and 11 should be reviewed and briefly processed. For homework, adult members should list several changes they have seen in their youth that they are most proud of.

Session Length: 120 minutes

Materials Needed: music, lyrics, and a music player

Handouts Needed (see Participant's Toolkit): "My Dream Life" and "Goals"

Group Format: Check In – Lesson – Processing – Songs – Processing – Check Out

Session 8: Youth and Parents/Guardians (Combined for Youth session 12)

Objective: The goal of this session is to celebrate family strength and the progress the youth and guardians/parents have made.

Session Length: 120 minutes

Materials Needed: music, lyrics, and a music player

Handouts Needed (see Participant's Toolkit): "Goals Wrap-Up"

Group Format: Check In – Songs – Processing – Awards – Check Out

Detailed Descriptions of H.Y.P.E. Sessions

The following sections provide detailed descriptions of each H.Y.P.E. sessions's activities and handouts. In addition, it lists useful references that can aid in group facilitation , and are recommended for potential facilitators. All handouts are available at www.letsgethype.com.

Session 1: You Don't Know My Struggle

Theme: History of rap music, H.Y.P.E., and Disruptive Behavior Disorders

Preparatory Material

Because every session includes discussions that focus on experiences with race, it is recommended that facilitators refer to the Glossary of race related terms found at the following link: www.hsp.org/default.aspx?id=397.

ICEBREAKERS

Name That Rapper. Group members will sit in a circle. The facilitator, who will serve as the "DJ," will play a portion of a rap song, and group members will attempt to guess the artist. No more than ten songs should be chosen for this icebreaker. Links to songs can be found at www.letsgethype.com. Facilitators may also divide the group into two competing teams to encourage peer interactions and increase group cohesion.

I'm Not a Biter, I'm a Writer. This activity will require group members to write their lyrics on the "I'm Not a Biter, I'm a Writer" handout provided in Part 4 of this book. Divide participants into two groups, and give them the following instructions: *"You and your group have 15 minutes to create a rap about 'unity'. After your time is up, your group will perform your song. There is only one requirement for song development and the group performance; you and your group members must make these decisions together."*
While group members are creating their songs and deciding who will perform them, they should be reminded

H.Y.P.E.
(Healing Young People through Empowerment)

to compromise when needed and work together. After each performance, group members should clap and offer encouragement to each other. This may aid in building group cohesion.

The facilitator should explain the "H.Y.P.E. Creed", including the call and response format. The facilitator must also explain the "Say influential person's name" portion of the creed, which requires members to say the name of a person they admire (e.g. a living or deceased family member, friend, mentor, entertainer, etc.). H.Y.P.E. members should understand that by saying the person's name, they are bringing that person's energy into the session. The facilitator(s) should further encourage each group member to lead the creed at least once over the 12 sessions.

Group members will review the "Disruptive Behavior Checklist (From DSM-IV-T-R)". Group members should identify the disruptive behaviors they've engaged in listed on this handout. The following process questions can be used to facilitate discussion among the group:
- *When did you first do the behaviors you identified on the checklist? (The facilitator can name the specific behavior.)*
- *Who were you with when you engaged in these activities?*
- *Were you ever caught doing these activities? What consequences did you have?*
- *Do you think your race made a difference in your engagement in these behaviors? Why or why not?*

Journal Topic 1: Talk about the disruptive behaviors from the checklist that you shared during the session, including how they have impacted your life.

Suggested topics for processing songs:

- Did you think about specific past experiences when you heard this song? Please share them.
- What feelings did you have when you heard this song?
- What has prevented you from changing behaviors that have led to negative consequences?
- What was going on in your life when you began doing the behaviors you identified on the checklist?
- What don't people understand about your struggle?
- How does a person's environment impact his actions?

Session 2: Buck the World (Part 1)

Theme: Defining anger and exploring depression – real talk

Preparatory Material

Social Cognitive Theory of Self-Efficacy by Frank Pajares

In order to gain an understanding of the social cognitive theory, the foundation of Session 2 and Session 3, facilitators should read this article, which can be found at the following link: http://www.des.emory.edu/mfp/eff.html.

H.Y.P.E.
(Healing Young People through Empowerment)

It includes and explains the concepts included in the theory, and provides an explanation for the Social Cognitive Model diagram listed on the "What is Anger? What is Depression? What is Sadness?" handout provided in Part 4 of this manual.

The following words are listed on the "What is Anger? What is Depression? What is Sadness?" handout in the Participant's Toolkit. The facilitator should first have group members define the three terms in their own words:

- *Anger*
- *Depression*
- *Sadness*

After each word is defined by the group, definitions from the World Wide Web, listed below should be read to the group by the facilitator or group members.

Definitions of **anger** on the Web:

- A strong emotion; a feeling that is oriented toward some real or supposed grievance; Anger is belligerence aroused by a real or supposed wrong. http://wordnetweb.princeton.edu/perl/webwn?s=anger&o2=&o0=1&o7=&o5=&o1=1&o6=&o4=&o3=&h=

- Anger is a (physiological and psychological) response to a perceived threat to self or important others' present, past, or future. The threat may appear to be real, discussed, or imagined. en.wikipedia.org/wiki/Anger

- A negative emotional reaction associated with other bad feelings such as fear, disgust, shame, irritability, outrage, hostility and possibly even violence. www.eubios.info/biodict.htm

Part 3: Facilitator's Guide

Definitions of **depression** on the Web:

- An illness that involves the body, mood, and thoughts that affect the way a person eats and sleeps, the way one feels about oneself, and the way one thinks about things. www.medterms.com/script/main/art.asp? articlekey=2947

- The depressed older child may sulk, get into trouble at school, be negative, grouchy, and feel misunderstood. Signs of depressive disorders in young people are often viewed as normal mood swings that are typical in this stage of life. Disruptive Behavior Disorders often accompany depression in adolescents. www.medicinenet. com/script/main/art.asp?articlekey=23376

- A state of unhappiness and hopelessness encarta. msn. com/ dictionary_1861603873/depression.html

Definitions of **sadness** on the Web:

- Emotions experienced when not in a state of well-being; Gloominess, the quality of excessive mournfulness and uncheerfulness http://wordnetweb.princeton.edu/ perl/webwn?s=sadness&o2=&o0=1&o7=&o5=&o1= 1&o6=&o4=&o3=&h=

- Affected with or marked by unhappiness, as that caused by affliction http://www.thefreedictionary.com/sadness
- A feeling or spell of dismally low spirits http://www. answers.com/topic/sadness

Also included on the "What is Anger? What is Depression? What is Sadness?" handout is the question listed below:

H.Y.P.E.
(Healing Young People through Empowerment)

- *How have issues related to oppression (e.g. racial profiling by law enforcement, differential treatment at school, or poor service at a business) influenced the strong emotions you've experienced?*

Group members will write and discuss their responses to this question. It may be beneficial for members to share their personal experiences with issues related to oppression.

Journal Topic 2: Rewrite the ending of an incident that led to negative consequences based on the information shared today.

Suggested topics for processing songs:

- Have you ever experienced any of the feelings described in this song? What triggered these feelings and how did you respond to them?
- How did you handle the strong feelings and difficult situations you went through?
- Please share a time when you experienced strong emotions as a result of being discriminated against?
- Does the social cognitive model fit your experiences? Why or why not?
- What role has your environment played in how you handled a conflict?
- Have you ever "lived every day like I'm gonna die?" How can this thinking affect your behavior and outlook on life?

Session 3: Buck the World (Part 2)

Preparatory Material

Group members are asked to write their answer and discuss the following question listed on the "What is Atonement" handout:

- *What is atonement?*

After members have been given adequate time to discuss this question, the facilitator should provide the definitions listed below:

Definitions of **atonement** on the Web:

- Compensation for a wrong; "we were unable to get satisfaction from the local store" http:// wordnetweb. princeton.edu/perl/webwn?s=atonement&o2= &o0=1&o7=&o5=&o1=1&o6=&o4=&o3=&h=

- Something done to make amends for wrongdoing www.thefreedictionary.com/atonement

- Reconciliation www.merriam-webster.com/dictionary/atonement

Also included in this session is an activity listed on the "Group Activity" handout in Part 4, in which vignettes or scenarios are presented that caused the main character to experience a strong emotion. It is recommended that group members volunteer to read the vignettes aloud. After Vignette 1 is read, the process questions listed below should be presented by the facilitator and discussed by group

H.Y.P.E.
(Healing Young People through Empowerment)

members. There are also Facilitator Tips included to aid the facilitator in guiding the discussion. After each process question is discussed, the facilitator should read the Vignette Conclusion also listed below. These steps should be repeated with Vignette 2.

Process Questions for Activity

* *Please explain these situations using the Social Cognitive Model of Behavior.*

    Facilitator tip: Marcela and J Dubb's interpretations of the comments made by the two authority figures were influenced by their personal concerns and immediate environment. They both had a history of engaging in inappropriate behavior and are now accustomed to receiving negative feedback as a result. They both jumped to a conclusion without listening to the messenger first. Encourage members to talk about times when they've felt the positive changes they've made have gone unnoticed.

* *What should s/he do now?*

    Facilitator tip: Encourage members to share how they may have responded to the scenarios. They can also offer specific solutions that they may not personally do.

* *What role might atonement play in this?*

    Facilitator tip: Have group members identify ways the characters could rectify these situations and possibly avoid negative consequences.

Vignette 1 Conclusion: J Dubb's mother was going to let him drive to the 6:00 game, but he interrupted her before she could say this. J Dubb falsely interpreted his mother's "no" (You can drive to a later game.) as "NO!" (I don't trust you and you're not mature enough to drive.)

Vignette 2 Conclusion: The support staff knew Marcela had been suspended and wanted to brighten her day by giving her a complement. Marcela, who was already frustrated and self-conscious about her hair and clothes, interpreted the comment as an insult rather than a compliment, and responded in a combative and oppositional manner.

Journal Topic 3: Talk about behaviors you would like to improve and how this change has already started.

Or...

Describe obstacles you may face as you work to improve aspects of yourself and your behavior.

Suggested topics for processing session songs:

- How have you dealt with pain in your life?
- What parts of changing your behavior concern you the most and/or may be harder?
- What steps have you begun to take to improve your life?
- What do you say you will quit most often? What prevents you from quitting?

H.Y.P.E.
(Healing Young People through Empowerment)

- How has oppression and prejudice impacted your behavior?
- How has society's view of Black boys and men impacted your personal factors and behavior?

Session 4: I'm Black

Preparatory Material

Because Session 4 focuses on group members' experiences with racism, and the history of discrimination against people of color in America, it is recommended that facilitators refer to the Glossary of race related terms found at the following link: www.hsp.org/default.aspx?id=397.

"Racism In Modern America" by Dinesh D'Souza
Additionally, it is recommended that facilitators read "Racism in Modern America," which explains the concepts of stereotype, discrimination, and race. In addition, D'Souza's article explores "America's 3 native and indigenous cultures," which is alleged to include Black Americans who came to the United States through the Trans-Atlantic slave trade. The author shares thought provoking ideas and concepts that may encourage discussion within the group. This article can be found at the following link: www.geocities.com/siliconvalley/hills/8908/rframe.htm.

The items listed below are on the "Pick a Family Member" handout, and should be written and discussed amongst H.Y.P.E. group members:

- *Pick a family member whose sacrifice has improved life for you today. What did they do?*
- *List two places or times when you have seen negative images of Black people.*

The chart on the <u>"Lifetime Chances of Going to State or Federal Prison for the First Time"</u> handout, shows the changes in one's chances of being incarcerated from 1974 to 2001. The chart data is divided by gender and racial groups. The facilitator should encourage group members to develop hypotheses to explain the differences between demographic groups, as well as the increased chance of going to prison from 1974 to 2001. If members do not identify mandatory minimum sentencing and discrimination in arrests and guilty convictions as possible explanations, the facilitator should pose these as hypotheses, and encourage members to debate them.

Also included on the <u>"Lifetime Chances of Going to State or Federal Prison for the First Time"</u> handout is the question listed below:

- *What is your responsibility in the legacy of Black America?*

This question will be discussed among group members, and they should also include written responses in the space provided on the handout. Answers may include: being a productive citizen, graduating from school, becoming a responsible father, or giving back to the community.

H.Y.P.E.
(Healing Young People through Empowerment)

Another handout, <u>"Notable Black Leaders of Today and the Past"</u>, is included in this session and lists several Black Politician's, scientists, business owners, and inventors. Group members should be encouraged to read the information listed on this handout outside of group.

Journal Topic 4: Describe how the sacrifices, struggles, and successes of your ancestors have helped you.

Or...

Talk about how you have been affected by racism.

Suggested topics for processing session songs:

- What have your experiences been like as a Black boy or man in this society?
- Have you ever been discriminated against? What role does discrimination play in being Black?
- How does society affect how you feel about being Black?
- How do you think your great-great grandparents wanted your life to be?
- How can learning about Black Americans in American history motivate you?
- Are there similarities between the treatment of Black people in the past and today? Explain.

Session 5: If My Homies Call

Group members will complete all three sections of the <u>"A Good Friend"</u> handout provided in Part 4. Afterwards,

they will compare and contrast their responses. The following are statements listed on "A Good Friend":

- *A good friend should...*
- *A good friend should not...*
- *When I was/am confronted with peer pressure I...*

Journal Topic 5: Talk about a time when you felt supported by your friend(s). Include a brief description of the circumstances and/or the actions taken by your friend(s).

Or...

Talk about a time when you suffered negative consequences as a result of giving in to peer pressure. Describe how you would do it differently.

Suggested topics for processing songs:

- How do you show your friends that you care?
- Have you ever been betrayed by a friend? What did they do?
- How have you been affected by peer pressure? How did you respond to it?
- What things are important to you and your friends?
- Share a time when your friends gave you positive advice. Share a time when your friends gave you negative advice.
- Share a negative experience you had with a friend.
- Share a time when your friend supported you.

H.Y.P.E.
(Healing Young People through Empowerment)

Session 6: I Really Miss My Homies
Theme: Death is a part of life...but it still hurts.

Preparatory Material

Because the focus of Session 6 is on grief and loss, it may be beneficial for facilitators to review information about the Kubler-Ross and Dr. Temes models at the following links:

- http://www.cancersurvivors.org/Coping/end%20term/stages.htm
- http://grief.com/the-five-stages-of-grief/,
- http://www.qcc.cuny.edu/Social Sciences/ppecorino/Deathand Dying_TEXT/Three-Stages-of-Grief.htm

After the songs are presented and processed, facilitators should read each stage of the Kubler-Ross model, listed on the "Grief Models and Activity" handout. Next, the Dr. Temes model of grief, also on this handout, should be read and explained.

Group members will then complete the activity listed on the "Grief Models and Activity" handout. To do this, they will identify an experience with grief or loss (e.g. death of a loved one, incarceration of a family member, or damage caused by a natural disaster or fire). Next members will name the feelings they had, and specify their strategies for coping. Finally, group members will identify how their experience fits with at least one of the models.

Part 3: Facilitator's Guide

The chart on the <u>"Leading Causes of Death"</u> handout should be reviewed by group members. With the facilitator's assistance, members will identify the similarities and differences between the leading causes of death for Black and White Americans. Members should then write their response to the following question also listed on this handout:

- *Why do you think there are differences in the causes of death between Black and White Americans?*

Journal Topic 6: Write a tribute to honor a loved one you have lost.

Or...

Talk about the emotions you experienced after your loss, and how you coped with the loss.

Suggested topics for processing songs:

- Has a friend or family member you were close to died?
- What emotions and feelings have you experienced as a result of your death/loss? How did you deal with the loss?
- What do you miss the most about the person you lost?
- What trait did you admire most in him/her?
- What would you like to tell the person you lost? Why?
- How did your life change after you lost someone close to you?

H.Y.P.E.
(Healing Young People through Empowerment)

- Did your view of death change? Why or why not? How did it change?
- Does the way someone dies impact the way you experience the loss? Why or why not?

Session 7: Dear Mama (Part 1)

Preparatory Material

"The Moynihan Report: Why are Black Families in Crisis?" by Daniel Patrick Moynihan

In order to gain an understanding of the impact of oppression on Black families, facilitators are encouraged to read this 1965 report, in which Daniel Patrick Moynihan argues that the roots of Black family problems lie in the dehumanization and legacy of slavery, growing urbanization, discrimination, and a tradition of matriarchy. This report can be found at the following link: www.children.smartlibrary.org/newinterface/segment.cfm?segment=1805

Answers to the first two questions on the "Family Traditions and Memories" handout should be written and discussed by group members, and are listed below:

- *A positive family memory or tradition*
- *A negative family memory or tradition*

Examples of positive traditions are holiday dinners, family reunions, college attendance, and having parties.

Examples of negative traditions are alcohol and drug abuse, incarceration, dropping out of school, and involvement in illegal activity.

The last two portions of the "Family Traditions and Memories" handout should be completed after session songs have been discussed, and are listed below:

- *I would like to improve my relationship with:*
- *Three goals I have for this relationship are:*

If a parent/guardian H.Y.P.E. group is included, group members should list their participating guardian as the person they'd like an improved relationship with. Likewise, the three goals should be geared towards the H.Y.P.E. youth and parent members' relationship. If a parent group is not included, or the participating guardian is a non-related temporary foster parent, group members should identify a family member with whom they are able to have face to face or written contact with.

The three goals for either scenario may include, but are not limited to the following: increasing written communication between one another, talking to each other uninterrupted for 30 minutes a week, eating one meal per week together, or saying "I love you" more.

Journal Topic 7: Talk about a negative family tradition/memory. How did you deal with it? How is it still affecting you?

H.Y.P.E.
(Healing Young People through Empowerment)
Suggested topics for processing songs:

- What family member are you closest to? What makes this relationship so special?
- What experiences have you had that were triggered by this song?
- How have you dealt with negative and painful family experiences?
- How have you coped with the abandonment of a close family member (i.e., father or mother)?
- How did your life change after your loved one left your life?

Session 8: Dear Mama (Part 2)
Theme: Moving our families in a positive direction, one step at a time.
Preparatory Material

If the H.Y.P.E. Parent group is conducted, family members should be included in this session, and facilitators should refer to the following reference:

Cody, P.S. (2006) Working with oppositional youths using Brief Strategic Family Therapy. In Franklin, C, Harris, M.B., & Allen-Meares, P. (Eds.), *The school services sourcebook: A guide for school-based professionals* (pp. 671–680). New York: Oxford University Press.

A summary of the material contained in this reference is listed below:

Brief Strategic Family Therapy (BSFT) Techniques are based on the fundamental concepts of system, structure, and strategy. Within the family *system* each member's behavior impacts the other member's, creating a system that functions within the larger system of society. A family's *structure* is the set of repeated patterns and interactions that are unique to each family. For example, a maladaptive family structure is one whose patterns continue though family member needs are not being met. The *strategy* concept includes a calculated set of intervention skills, which are direct, problem-oriented, and practical. This theory is the basis for the activity at the end of the session, which requires youth and guardian members to develop strategies for improving their relationships. Each member's evaluation of the system and structure will lead to the development of a strategy.

It is also recommended that facilitator's review the book, *Slavery by Another Name*, which among other things, chronicles the intergenerational struggles of Black families, and the impact of discrimination.

Blackmon, D.A. (2008) *Slavery by another name: The reinslavement of Black Americans from the Civil War to World War II.* New York: Doubleday.

At the start of the session, group members should write and discuss amongst each other, their thoughts about the following statement on the "My Family..." handout:

- *Oppression has impacted my family by:*

Some themes that should be interjected by the facilitator if participants do not mention them include: disparity in

H.Y.P.E.
(Healing Young People through Empowerment)

drug laws, housing, unemployment, and the longstanding implications of slavery/Jim Crow laws to name a few.

If parent group members are included, H.Y.P.E. youth and guardian members will break into dyads to discuss the goals and areas of improvement identified during Session 7. After no more than 15 minutes of discussion time, the youth/guardian teams will share their ideas with the rest of the group. Everyone can contribute thoughts and suggestions about the team's ideas, which the youth/guardian dyad will write on a poster board. The poster board may include relationship goals, long-term objectives, strategy details, and helpful techniques they and the other group members discussed during the session.

If family members are not included, group members should write and share their responses to the following statements listed on the "My Family..." handout:

- *I can have a positive influence on my family by:*
- *I can have a negative influence on my family by:*

Examples of positive influence include excelling academically, obeying authority figures, working towards positive goals, and complimenting others. Negative influence examples include engaging in illegal behavior, school truancy, and being mean to others. Group members should also be encouraged to share personal examples of times when they've noticed their positive and negative influence on other family members.

Journal Topic 8: Describe a good family memory, including your feelings at the time, those involved, and the role you played.

Suggested topics for processing songs:

- What new tradition would you like to introduce to your family?
- What would you like to hear a family member who has hurt you in the past say?
- What positive change can you make in your family (e.g., setting a good example for younger relatives)?
- How has your family's presence or absence impacted your life? How do you think this presence/absence could impact your relationships in the future?
- What role has extended family, including family friends and foster families, played in your life?

Session 9: Git Up, Git Out and Git Somethin (Part 1)
Theme: Lavish living later is the result of planning and hard hustling today

Facilitators should encourage group members to identify positive and negative short-term and long-term consequences when responding to the following statements listed on the "Consequences" handout:

- *List two short-term consequences of an illegal hustle.*

H.Y.P.E.
(Healing Young People through Empowerment)

> * *List two long-term consequences of an illegal hustle.*

"Illegal hustles" are illegal activities people engage in to earn money. As the group members respond to these statements, the facilitator should challenge members to identify an individual they know personally, who has retired from an illegal hustle with enough money to survive long-term, without: being physically harmed, incarcerated, or experiencing any negative consequence while engaging in this activity. It is highly unlikely that any member will know anyone that meets these criteria, although one or two may initially reply affirmatively to this question. Group members should be encouraged to briefly talk about this.

Members should then review and discuss the table on the "Consequences" handout that lists examples of skills required to sell drugs and steal cars, as well as comparable legal hustles. Facilitators should then encourage group members to identify a third hustle, skills necessary to complete it, and comparable legal hustles, orally as a group.

After the session songs are reviewed and processed, group members should begin the activity that includes the "Snapshot of Adult Life," "Vignette A & B," and "H.Y.P.E. Monthly Budget" handouts listed in Part 4.

The "Snapshot of Adult Life" handout includes a chart that shows the average annual income for males and females with different educational levels. After a brief discussion about the years it takes to attain the various degrees and income differences, members should identify and share the highest educational level they are willing to attain with the rest of the group.

Group members should be encouraged to choose the education level based on the amount of time they are willing to attend school, and not just the income level. It is recommended that only a couple minutes be allotted to selecting an educational level.

Once all members have identified their educational level, the facilitator (or volunteer group members) will read Vignette A from the "Vignette A & B" handout, for the educational levels selected by group members. Vignette A will describe the job, income, fringe benefits, and responsibilities. After Vignette A is read for each group members' educational level, they should write their income level at the top of the "H.Y.P.E. Monthly Budget" handout. Facilitators will then read each line item listed on the "H.Y.P.E. Monthly Budget" handout, and members will write the amount they believe they will spend on the item during the month. For some items, youth may not wish to spend anything; however this should be processed to determine how realistic this is. Additionally, facilitators will likely be required to provide youth with estimated costs for many items (e.g. rent/mortgage, utilities, car payment, insurance, etc.). After all of the items have been explained, and youth have inputted costs, the facilitator will read Vignette B from the "Vignette A & B" handout.

H.Y.P.E.
(Healing Young People through Empowerment)

The cost included in Vignette B should be added to the "H.Y.P.E. Monthly Budget" handout.

With the inclusion of Vignette B, youth should have completed the "H.Y.P.E. Monthly Budget" handout. The facilitator will then tally the amount of money each youth will have at the end of the month from the lowest to the highest education level. This is done by the facilitator inputting the monthly income for a youth into a calculator, and deducting each of the expenses, read orally by the group member. This portion of the activity will likely take about 30 minutes. If time remains when this is completed, group members should share aspects of the activity that surprised them the most.

Journal Topic 9: Talk about the short- and long-term consequences of an illegal hustle.

Suggested topics for processing songs:

- Of the all disruptive behaviors you've engaged in, which have led to the harshest consequences? What can you do (or have you done) to avoid such behaviors and consequences now and in the future?
- What would you NOT want your life as an adult to look like? Why?
- What makes selling drugs and/or other illegal hustles addictive?
- How does your environment impact the choices you have for your future, particularly with employment?

Session 10: Git Up, Git Out, and Git Somethin (Part 2)

Theme: Learning from those who have walked down this path before us

Preparatory Material

Heavy Time for Drug Lightweights by Debra J. Saunders

In 1986, Congress passed the Anti-Drug Abuse Act, which included a mandatory minimum sentence of five years for selling 5 grams of crack cocaine. Within this same act, 100 times more powder cocaine would warrant the same 5-year mandatory minimum sentence, at 500 grams.

The U.S. Sentencing Commission found that in 2000, 84% of federal crack cocaine offenders were Black, while only 5% were White. This article details the fight within Congress to erase the differences in crack cocaine and powder cocaine sentencing, which was led by then Senator Joe Biden. Also detailed is the impact of this disparity in sentencing on "kingpins" versus low level drug dealers. This article can be found at the following link: http://caglepost.com/column/Deb+Saunders/4339/Heavy+Time+for+Drug+Lightweights.html

How Does Conspiracy Law Work?

In 1988 Congress passed another Anti-Drug Law. One of the provisions was urged by the Department of Justice to close a loophole in a previous act. The change, which was to apply to the mandatory sentences of 1986, was intended

H.Y.P.E.
(Healing Young People through Empowerment)

for high level traffickers and anyone who was a member of a drug trafficking conspiracy. The effect of this amendment was to make everyone in a conspiracy liable for every act of the conspiracy, from the doorman of a crack house to the leader of the operation.

After the conspiracy amendment was enacted, the prison population swelled, and within 6 years, the number of drug cases in federal prisons increased by 300%. From 1986 to 1998 it was up by 450%. This article can be found at the following link: http://www.pbs.org/wgbh/pages/frontline/shows/snitch/primer/

If guest speakers are not included in this session, group members will be given no more than 10 minutes to complete the first statement on the "My Dream Life" handout:

- *In my dream life I…*

This activity should be presented by the facilitators asking the following:

> *"Thinking as big as you can what would your dream life look like? What would you do in your dream life? Where would you live? No dream is too big."*

It is likely that at least one group member will have significant difficulty completing this task. These youth should be asked to think about the life they wouldn't want to have, and then identify life experiences that would be the opposite of that.

After group members have completed the first statement, facilitators will direct them to answer the second statement:

- *I can make this dream a reality by...*

Group members should identify actions including attending school regularly, volunteering for a company or organization, finding a job, practicing a skill, or changing their social circle.

If guest panels will not be included, the facilitator can also bring biographies and information about people who have made changes in their lives, going on to lead successful lives.

If guest panels are included, session songs should be played and processed at the beginning of the session. Due to time limitations, it is recommended that panels include no more than three people. These individuals may talk briefly about relevant elements of their past, their current lives including employment, educational attainment, and plans for the future.

Panel 1, which includes individuals currently dealing with negative consequences of their actions, will convene for 30 minutes. Panel guests will identify the actions that led to the consequence they were given (e.g. juvenile/adult incarceration, probation, or injuries to themselves or people they were close to), and how their lives changed.
Panel 2 will begin right after this panel ends, and will last about 35-40 minutes. These panel members will talk about the steps they took to get to their position in life. Group members should be encouraged to ask panel members questions.

H.Y.P.E.
(Healing Young People through Empowerment)

Journal Topic 10: Talk about what you are willing to do to make your dreams come true.

Suggested topics for processing songs:

- Talk about the differences between "living everyday like you're going to die" and "living everyday like you're going to live."
- Do you have a plan for realizing the American Dream? What resources do you think could help you achieve your American Dream?
- What sacrifices are you willing to make to achieve your goals?
- What can be your motivation for accomplishing your goals? How can you tap into this?
- How do you think your neighborhood would be different if the people who "made it" didn't leave?
- Name some factors that have prevented you from changing behaviors that have led to negative consequences in the past?

Session 11: We've Got to Plan, Plot, Strategize
Theme: Using the lessons I've learned to guide my future

Preparatory Material
Mentor Program. Facilitators, who wish to include a mentorship program, must insure mentoring programs with openings are available and relatively close to group

members' residences. Ideally, group members would have several mentorship options to choose from, however as long as the first criteria is met for at least one mentorship program, H.Y.P.E. referrals can be initiated. After Session 1, the facilitator should develop a list of possible referrals, to be presented to members during Session 11. After session songs are processed, group members who wish to participate in a mentorship program should identify the one they're interested in. Before a final referral is made, parents/guardian permission for interested group members must first be obtained. Several national and local referral sources that may offer mentorship programs in your local area are listed below.

Possible Referral Sources
- Local colleges and universities
- Local churches
- Local 100 Black Men of America Chapter
- Local business owners
- Association of Black Psychologist (ABPsi)
- National Society of Black Engineers (NSEB)
- National Black MBA Association (NBMBAA)
- National Association of Black Journalists (NABJ)
- The Urban League
- National Association for the Advancement of Colored People (NAACP)
- The Optimist Club
- Masonic Organizations
- Order of the Eastern Star
- Greek Organizations
- The Ludacris Foundation
- K.I.N.G. Foundation

H.Y.P.E.
(Healing Young People through Empowerment)

- – Association of Black Doctors
- – Association of Black Physicians
- – National Dental Association
- – National Organization for the Professional Advancement of Black Chemists and Chemical Engineers (NOBCChE)
- – Association of Black Health-System Pharmacists
- – Black Lawyers Association

Upon introduction of the "Goals" handout, the facilitator will say:

> *"We are nearing the end of our journey together, and we have talked a lot about your past, and you've started to think about your dream life. Now, I want you to imagine yourself one year from today, and identify a goal that you would like to accomplish by then. Please consider a realistic short-term goal that you can accomplish within the next 365 days. What steps will you need to take to fulfill this goal?"*

Group members should then write and discuss their responses for the following statements listed on the "Goals" handout:

- *My 1 year goal is...*
- *To fulfill this goal I...*

Some group members may find it difficult to formulate a goal. These individuals should be encouraged to think about concrete, non-complex goals (e.g. remaining in school, staying in contact with a positive role model or friend, avoiding contact with law enforcement).

Part 3: Facilitator's Guide

To introduce the next section, the facilitator can say:

"Now that you've thought about the next year, I want you to think about your life five years from now? What will you be doing? Where will you be living? What will you need to do to fulfill this goal?"

After group members have completed the year one portion of the handout, they should write and discuss their responses to the following:
- *My 5 year goal is...*
- *To fulfill this goal I...*

If group members have difficulty with this portion of the "Goals" handout, encourage them to think about how they would not want their lives to be five years from now. From here, as a means of goal development, members should identify one area of their lives that can be changed or improved, or an accomplishment they wish to realize within five years.

Journal Topic 11: **Share the reasons you are hopeful and why you believe your goals and dreams should come true.**

Suggested topics for processing songs:

- What are your biggest fears about working towards and achieving your dreams?
- What behaviors do you need to improve to be sure you achieve your goals? Which have you already started to improve?

H.Y.P.E.
(Healing Young People through Empowerment)

- What role could society play in your journey towards accomplishing your goals?
- How will racism and oppression affect your journey towards accomplishing your goals?
- Who can be a source of support as you work to accomplish your goals? How can you access them? What has kept you from reaching out to them in the past?

Session 12: I Remember
Theme: Celebrating the progress we've made as we continue to progress

If a formal parent/guardian group was formed, youth and guardian members should break into dyads to identify changes they've seen in each other. Youth and guardian members will then complete the "Goals Wrap-Up" item together which states the following:

- *List three things you are willing to do to continue to fulfill the goals you named in Session 11*

After about 15 minutes in the dyads, the group will come together, and the dyads will share their response to "Goals Wrap-Up."

If a formal parent/guardian group was not formed, the "Goals Wrap-Up" handout will be written and then discussed by group members individually.

After the initial activity is completed, group members should begin eating the food brought in for the party. The session songs will be presented and processed while everyone eats. Certificates will be awarded after the final song is processed.

If the Mentor Program will be included, group members should be provided with the contact information for the program they are being referred to before the group ends for the final time.

Suggested topics for processing songs:

- What changes have you seen in yourself (and family member(s) if program is included)? What are you most proud of?
- What behaviors are you willing to continue to work on in an effort to fulfill your ultimate goals?

H.Y.P.E.
(Healing Young People through Empowerment)

Part 4: Participants Toolkit

H.Y.P.E. CREED

I believe in myself
I will accomplish my goals
I know that I have gifts
And it is my job to share these gifts
With my family
With my community
And with the world

I will remain true to the hip-hop culture
And will adopt the virtue of peace,
which our community was founded on

I am learning that we all make mistakes
And it is my responsibility to learn
from my mistakes
I ask that (*Say influential person's name*)
walk with me during this session
Throughout the next week, or until
our group meets again
Share with me those positive traits
That I so admire within you

H.Y.P.E.
(Healing Young People through Empowerment)

Session 1: You Don't Know My Struggle

Theme: History of rap music, H.Y.P.E., and Disruptive Behavior Disorders

I'm Not a Biter, I'm a Writer

_____

_____

_____

_____

_____

_____

_____

_____

_____

_____

_____

_____

_____

_____

_____

_____

_____

_____

_____

_____

H.Y.P.E.
(Healing Young People through Empowerment)

BRIEF HISTORY OF HIP-HOP CULTURE

- Hip-hop culture was created in the early 1970's by Black and Latino youth in New York City.
- The four elements of hip-hop culture are rapping/mceeing, breakdancing, graffiti, and DJing.
- Jamaican born DJ Kool Here, who immigrated to New York City in the late 1960's, is known as "the godfather of rap."
- DJ Kool Here introduced the Jamaican tradition of "toasting," which involves rhyming over reggae music. He also introduced the idea of using two turntables to alternate between two songs while freestyling toasting rhymes.
- In 1979, "Rapper's Delight" by the Sugar Hill Gang became the first rap recording. This song introduced the rest of America to rap music, which soon became the voice of young Black America.
- Rap and hip-hop culture lets its followers tell their stories and communicate their dreams, frustrations, aggression, and show their creativity.
- Today, rap is one of the most popular forms of music among young people in America, and it has influenced every part of American culture.
- A thriving hip-hop culture can also be found in countries all over the world, including France, Nigeria, Japan, and Israel. Hip-hop has erased all boundaries of race, nationality, and language.
- Hip-hop culture is an important influence in the lives of most young Black American males. 97% of Black males say they "like" rap music.

DISRUPTIVE BEHAVIOR CHECKLIST
(From the DSM-IV-T-R)

o Aggression to people and animals

- often bullies, threatens, or intimidates others
- often initiates physical fights
- has used a weapon that can cause serious physical harm to others
- has been physically cruel to people and/or animals
- has stolen while confronting a victim

o Destruction of property

- has deliberately engaged in fire setting with the intention of causing serious damage
- has deliberately destroyed others' property (other than by fire setting)

o Deceitfulness or theft

- has broken into someone's home, building, or car
- often lies to obtain goods or favors or to avoid obligations (cons others)
- has stolen items of nontrivial value without confronting a victim (shoplifting, forgery)

o Serious violations of rules

- often stays out at night despite parental prohibitions (beginning before age 13)
- has run away from home overnight at least twice
- is often truant from school (beginning before age 13)

H.Y.P.E.
(Healing Young People through Empowerment)

Journal Topic 1: Talk about the disruptive behaviors from the checklist that you shared during the session, including how they have impacted your life.

_____

_____

_____

_____

_____

_____

_____

_____

_____

_____

_____

_____

_____

_____

_____

_____

_____

_____

_____

_____

Session 2: Buck the World (Part 1)

Theme: Defining anger and exploring depression – real talk

H.Y.P.E.
(Healing Young People through Empowerment)

"What is Anger? What is Depression? What is Sadness?"

What is Anger? What is Depression? What is Sadness?

_____

_____

_____

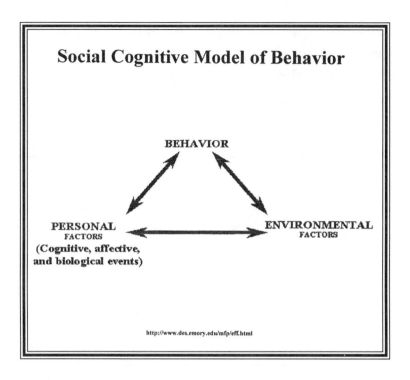

How have issues related to oppression (e.g. racial profiling by law enforcement or poor service at a business) influenced the strong emotions you've experienced?

_____

_____

_____

_____

_____

H.Y.P.E.
(Healing Young People through Empowerment)

Journal Topic 2: Rewrite the ending of an incident that led to negative consequences based on the information shared today.

_____

_____

_____

_____

_____

_____

_____

_____

_____

_____

_____

_____

_____

_____

_____

_____

_____

_____

_____

_____

_____

_____

Session 3: Buck the World (Part 2)

Theme: Developing an arsenal to constructively respond to strong emotions

H.Y.P.E.
(Healing Young People through Empowerment)

"What is atonement?"

_____

_____

_____

_____

_____

_____

_____

_____

_____

_____

_____

_____

_____

_____

_____

_____

_____

_____

_____

_____

_____

_____

_____

Part 4: Participant's Toolkit

"Group Activity"

Vignette 1

J Dubb is a 16 year-old guy who is currently in the 10th grade. He works at McDonald's part-time.

On his recent report card, his grades improved from D's to B's and C's. As a result of his increased efforts, his mother has given him more privileges, which include driving her car and hanging out with his friends.

Today is the last day of the big Round Robin basketball tournament that has been going on for the past two days. There are three matches per day, and J Dubb figured he'd ask his mom if he could use the car for the first game, since he would be home early and she couldn't have a reason to trip. When he made this request his mother said no, and J Dubb instantly stormed out of the room saying, "Why won't you let me grow up? I'm trying to change, Ma, but what's the point if you won't trust me?"

Vignette 2

Marcela is a 14 year-old girl, and this is her first day returning to school after being suspended for two days (she walked out of the classroom too many times). The school year is coming to an end, and due to her behavior management difficulties during this time, the support staff has gotten to know her pretty well.

Marcela didn't have time to fix her hair, and then last period she realized she had forgotten to bring her make-up assignment. As she is walking to her next class, frustrated

H.Y.P.E.
(Healing Young People through Empowerment)

and angry, the smiling support staff in the hallway says, "'Cela, you look nice today!" Marcela instantly "rolls" her eyes and says, "You don't have to rub it in, smart ass."

Process Questions for Activity

- Please explain these situations using the Social Cognitive Behavioral Model.

- What should s/he do now?

- What role might atonement play in this?

Journal Topic 2: Talk about behaviors you would like to improve and how this change has already started. Or...

Describe obstacles you may face as you work to improve aspects of yourself and your behavior.

_____

_____

_____

_____

_____

_____

_____

_____

_____

_____

Session 4: I'm Black

Theme: Present day empowerment through exploration of the past

H.Y.P.E.
(Healing Young People through Empowerment)

"Pick a Family Member"

Pick a family member whose sacrifice has improved life for you today. What did they do?

_____

_____

_____

_____

_____

_____

_____

_____

_____

_____

_____

List two places or times when you have seen negative images of Black people.

1. _____

2. _____

"Lifetime Chances of Going to State or Federal prison For the First Time"

Lifetime Chances of Going to State or Federal Prison for the First Time

Race	1974	1991	2001
White male	2.2%	4.4%	5.9%
White female	0.2%	0.5%	0.9%
Black male	13.4%	29.4%	32.3%
Black female	1.1%	3.6%	5.6%
Latino male	4.0%	11.1%	17.2%
Latina female	0.4%	1.5%	2.2%

Source: Bonczar, T. P. (2003). Prevalence of Imprisonment in the U.S. Population, 1974-2001. Washington, DC: Bureau of Justice Statistics, August.

What is your responsibility in the legacy of Black America?

_____

_____

_____

_____

_____

_____

H.Y.P.E.
(Healing Young People through Empowerment)
"Notable Black Leaders of Today and the Past"

CIVIL RIGHTS LEADERS	GOVERNMENT OFFICIALS
Ralph Abernathy, civil rights leader	Shirley Anita Chisholm, American politician
Daisy Bates, civil rights leader	Tom Bradley, American politician
Black Panthers, U.S. Black militant party	Carol Moseley Braun, U.S. senator
Julian Bond, U.S. civil rights leader	Ralph Bunche, U.S. government official and United Nations diplomat
Stokely Carmichael, radical civil rights leader	President Barack Obama, first Black U.S. President
Shirley Chisholm, U.S. Congresswoman	James Armistead, American Revolution patriot
Charles Hamilton Houston, civil rights lawyer	Paul Cuffe, U.S. seaman, philanthropist
Eldridge Cleaver, American social activist	Benjamin O. Davis, Sr., American general
Medgar Evers, civil rights leader	David Dinkins, political leader
Malcolm X, civil rights leader and revolutionary	General Benjamin O. Davis, Jr., American air force general
Marcus Garvey, Black nationalist leader	Joycelyn Elders, U.S. Surgeon General
Greensboro Four, civil rights activist	A. Leon Higginbotham, Jr., prominent federal judge and historian
SCIENTISTS AND INVENTORS	**SCHOLARS AND EDUCATORS**
Archibald Alphonso Alexander, design and construction engineer	John Mercer Langston, educator, public official, diplomat
Benjamin Banneker, American intellectual and scientist	Kenneth B. Clark, American educator and psychologist
Herman Russell Branson, physicist	John Hope Franklin, American historian
George Washington Carver, American agricultural chemist	Marcus Garvey, American proponent of Black nationalism
Jewel Plummer Cobb, biologist, physiologist	Inez Beverly Prosser, first Black female psychologist in America
David Crosthwait, Jr., engineer, inventor	W. E. B. Du Bois, American author and teacher
Charles Richard Drew, physician	John Johnson, publisher
Clarence L. Elder, engineer and inventor	Ernest Everest Just, biologist, educator
Philip Emeagwali, computer scientist, mathematician	Archibald H. Grimke, African American author and crusader for Black advancement
Evan Forde, oceanographer	Maulana Karenga, scholar
Lloyd Hall, chemist	Mary McLeod Bethune, American educator
Mae Jemison, astronaut, physician	Richard Gordon Hatcher, law professor, politician

Journal Topic 4: Describe how the sacrifices, struggles, and successes of your ancestors have helped you. Or...

Talk about how you have been influenced by racism.

_____

_____

_____

_____

_____

_____

_____

_____

_____

_____

_____

_____

_____

_____

_____

_____

_____

_____

H.Y.P.E.
(Healing Young People through Empowerment)

Session 5: If My Homies Call

Theme: Let's talk about friends, enemies, and peer pressure

"A Good Friend"

A Good Friend Should . . .

1. _____

2. _____

3. _____

A Good Friend Should Not . . .

1. _____

2. _____

3. _____

When I Was/Am Confronted with Peer Pressure I . . .

1. _____

2. _____

3. _____

H.Y.P.E.
(Healing Young People through Empowerment)

Journal Topic 5: Talk about a time when you felt supported by your friend(s). Include a brief description of the circumstances and/or the actions taken by your friend(s). Or...

Talk about a time when you suffered negative consequences as a result of giving in to peer pressure. Describe how you would do it differently.

_____

_____

_____

_____

_____

_____

_____

_____

_____

_____

_____

_____

_____

_____

_____

_____

_____

Session 6: I Really Miss My Homies

Theme: Death is a part of life…but it still hurts.

H.Y.P.E.
(Healing Young People through Empowerment)
"Grief Models and Activity"

http://www.cancersurvivors.org/Coping/end%20term/stages.htm

The stages Kubler-Ross identified are:

Denial (This isn't *happening* to me!)

Anger (Why is this happening to *me*?)

Bargaining (I promise I'll be a better person *if...*)

Depression (I don't *care* anymore.)

Acceptance (*I'm ready* for whatever comes.)

Dr. Roberta Temes Model

describes three particular types of behavior

exhibited by those suffering from grief and loss. They are:

Numbness (mechanical functioning and social insulation)

Disorganization (intensely painful feelings of loss)

Reorganization (re-entry into a more "normal" social life)

Experience_____

_____

Feelings_____

_____

Coping_____

_____

Describe your experience using at least one of the two models

_____

_____

158

Part 4: Participant's Toolkit

"Leading Causes of Death"

The following table shows that the ten leading causes of death for Black and White Americans are similar, although they occur at different rates within each population. The unique causes in each top ten list are highlighted.

10 Leading Causes of Death (Both Sexes, All Ages)	
African American	**White**
1. Heart Disease	1. Heart Disease
2. Cancer	2. Cancer
3. Cerebrovascular Disease (Stroke)	3. Cerebrovascular Disease (Stroke)
4. Accidents	4. Respiratory Disease (COPD)
5. Diabetes	5. Accidents
6. Homicide	6. Pneumonia and Influenza
7. Pneumonia and Influenza	7. Diabetes
8. Respiratory Disease (COPD)	**8. Suicide**
9. HIV (AIDS)	**9. Liver Disease**
10. Conditions originating in the perinatal period (period shortly before/after birth)	**10. Nephritis, Nephrotic Syndrome and Nephrosis**

Source: CDC, National Vital Statistics Report, Vol. 48, No. 11, July 24, 2000 (www.cdc.gov/nchs/data/nvsr/nvsr48/nvs48_11.pdf)

Why do you think there are differences in the causes of death between Black and White Americans?

_____

_____

_____

_____

_____

_____

H.Y.P.E.
(Healing Young People through Empowerment)

Journal Topic 6: Write a tribute to honor a loved one you have lost.

Or...

Talk about the emotions you experienced after your loss, and how you coped with the loss.

_____

_____

_____

_____

_____

_____

_____

_____

_____

_____

_____

_____

_____

_____

_____

_____

_____

_____

Session 7: Dear Mama (Part 1)

Theme: Exploring my family's past in an effort to improve my family's future

H.Y.P.E.
(Healing Young People through Empowerment)
"Family Traditions and Memories"

A positive family memory or tradition_____

_____

A negative family memory or tradition_____

_____

I would like to improve my relationship with_____

_____

Three goals I have for this relationship are:

1._____

2._____

3._____

Journal Topic 7: Talk about a negative family tradition/memory. How did you deal with it? How is it still affecting you?

_____

_____

_____

_____

_____

_____

_____

_____

_____

_____

_____

_____

_____

_____

_____

_____

_____

_____

_____

_____

_____

_____

H.Y.P.E.
(Healing Young People through Empowerment)

Session 8: Dear Mama (Part 2)

Theme: Moving our families in a positive direction, one step at a time.

"My Family…"

Oppression has impacted my family by_____

_____

_____

_____

_____

I can have a positive influence on my family by_____

_____

_____

_____

_____

I can have a negative influence on my family by_____

_____

_____

_____

_____

H.Y.P.E.
(Healing Young People through Empowerment)

Journal Topic 8: Describe a good family memory, including your feelings at the time, those involved, and the role you played.

_____

_____

_____

_____

_____

_____

_____

_____

_____

_____

_____

_____

_____

_____

_____

_____

_____

_____

_____

_____

_____

Session 9: Git Up, Git Out and Git Somethin (Part 1)

Theme: Lavish living later is the result of planning and hard hustling today

H.Y.P.E.
(Healing Young People through Empowerment)

"Consequences"

List two short-term consequences of an illegal hustle.

_____

_____

_____

_____

List two long-term consequences of an illegal hustle.

_____

_____

_____

_____

Examples of Hustle	Examples of Skills Required	Some Comparable Hustles
Selling drugs	Sales, inventory, accounting, budgeting, understanding forms of measurement, supervision, marketing	Salesman, business owner accountant, marketing, barber
Stealing cars	Being aware of your surroundings, basic mechanics of a car, using your hands, being efficient	Plumber, welder, woodworker, business owner, barber

Part 4: Participant's Toolkit

"Snapshot of Adult Life"

This table shows the average annual income for males and females with different educational levels. On average, individuals with higher educational levels tend to have larger incomes, while those with lower educational levels make less money.

Average Annual Income (in dollars), 2004		
Educational Level	Male	Female
Less than 9th grade	22,070	14,008
High school		
9th to 12th grade (no diploma)	22,795	13,519
High school graduate (includes equivalency)	34,050	21,923
College		
Some college, no degree	37,561	22,896
Associate degree	44,130	29,208
Bachelor's degree	63,753	38,766
Master's degree	84,017	50,547
Professional degree	137,050	70,812
Doctorate degree	104,848	68,191
Bachelor's degree or more (total)	75,719	43,853

Real Estate Market Data	United States
Average Home Price	$173,585
Median Rental Price	$471

Source: U.S. Bureau of the Census.

H.Y.P.E.
(Healing Young People through Empowerment)

H.Y.P.E. MONTHLY INCOME

	Total monthly income
HOUSING	Actual Cost
Mortgage or rent	
Phone	
Electricity	
Gas	
Water and sewer	
Cable	
Waste removal	
Maintenance or repairs	
Supplies (e.g. tissue, cleaning products, etc.)	
Other	
Subtotals	
TRANSPORTATION	Actual Cost
Vehicle payment	
Bus/taxi fare	
Insurance	
Fuel	
Maintenance	
Other	
Subtotals	
FOOD	Actual Cost
Groceries	
Dining out	
Subtotals	
PERSONAL CARE	Actual Cost
Hair/nails	
Clothing	
Dry cleaning	
Health club	
Other	
Subtotals	

	Actual Cost
ENTERTAINMENT	Actual Cost
Video/DVD	
CDs	
Movies	
Concerts	
Sporting events	
Plays	
Night Clubs	
Other	
Other	
Subtotals	
LEGAL	Actual Cost
Attorney	
Alimony	
Payments on lien or judgment	
Other	
Subtotals	
SAVINGS/ INVESTMENTS	Actual Cost
Retirement account	
Investment account	
Other	
Subtotals	
INSURANCE	Actual Cost
Home	
Health	
Life	
Subtotals	

170

Part 4: Participant's Toolkit

"Vignette A & B"

Vignette A	Vignette B
Less than high school or high school diploma (no trade/skills) – You are 22 years old, currently employed at a local Family Buck store, working 40 hours/week for minimum wage, and are bringing home $800 per month. You do not have health benefits through your job because you have only been employed at Family Buck for 3 months, so several times a year you must go to the welfare office to ensure that you receive your Medicaid. Though your income is limited, you make too much to money to receive Food Stamps. You do not receive any paid time off.	**Less than high school or high school diploma (no trade/skills)** – Last week you were sick and missed four straight days of work, so your check is significantly less. Additionally, you must repay your loan of $150 at the local Check My Cash loan office.
Associate Degree – You are 22 years old and currently employed at a community health center as an assistant office manager. You work 40 hours/week and bring home about $1600 per month. You receive full benefits from your job and one week per year for unpaid vacation/sick leave.	**Associate Degree** – Your car has started running poorly. You don't know what's wrong, so you have a diagnostic check run on it. The results of the check suggest your repair work will cost about $200, which gives you a total bill of $295.
Bachelor Degree – You are 22 years old and currently employed at the America County Juvenile Detention Center, where your annual salary is $38,900 ($3241/month). You have two weeks of paid vacation/sick leave per year, and can attend paid conferences once a month.	**Bachelor Degree** – You recently bought a house, which requires more repair work than you anticipated, and the fund you set aside to cover the cost is running out. The latest thing to go out is the water heater, and a halfway decent replacement is $500.
Master's Degree – You are 25 years old and a new AT&T technology department employee. Your annual salary is $51,000 ($4250/month), and your employee package includes health/dental benefits, a discounted landline, cable, DSL, and cell phone. You have two weeks paid vacation and one week paid sick leave per year, which will roll over. You also have free skills training in your area of choice (i.e., management, human resources).	**Master's Degree** – Three years ago you bought a beautiful golden retriever that instantly became part of your family. Last night, the dog tried to jump over your backyard fence and was cut severely by the wires. You rush your "baby" to the vet's office and rack up a bill of $650.
Professional or Doctorate Degree – You are 29 years old and a newly licensed psychologist. When you combine the income you receive from your private practice and other business ventures, you will bring in about $90,000 ($7500/month) this year. Because you are in private practice, you are able to make your own schedule, and are virtually your own boss; thus you can determine your vacation time, hours, etc.	**Professional or Doctorate Degree** – For the past year, you have been a big source of financial support for your parents, who live several states away. Recently, your mother called you to report that she hit a pothole, and three tires were flattened. You immediately wire $700, at a cost of about $800, to your mother.

H.Y.P.E.
(Healing Young People through Empowerment)

Journal Topic 9: Talk about the short- and long-term consequences of an illegal hustle.

_____

_____

_____

_____

_____

_____

_____

_____

_____

_____

_____

_____

_____

_____

_____

_____

_____

_____

_____

_____

_____

_____

Session 10: Git Up, Git Out, and Git Somethin (Part 2)

Theme: Learning from those who have walked down this path before us

H.Y.P.E.
(Healing Young People through Empowerment)

"My Dream Life"

In my dream life I...

_____

_____

I can make this dream a reality by...

_____

_____

Journal Topic 10: Talk about what you are willing to do to make your dreams come true.

_____

_____

_____

_____

_____

_____

_____

_____

_____

_____

_____

_____

_____

_____

_____

_____

_____

_____

_____

_____

_____

_____

Session 11: We've Got to Plan, Plot, Strategize

Theme: Using the lessons I've learned to guide my future

"GOALS"

My 1 year goal is_____

_____

_____

To fulfill this goal I_____

_____

_____

_____

My 5-year goal is_____

_____

_____

_____

To fulfill this goal I_____

_____

_____

_____

_____

H.Y.P.E.
(Healing Young People through Empowerment)

Journal Topic 11: Share the reasons you are hopeful and why you believe your goals and dreams should come true.

_____

_____

_____

_____

_____

_____

_____

_____

_____

_____

_____

_____

_____

_____

_____

_____

_____

_____

_____

_____

_____

Session 12: I Remember

Theme: Celebrating the progress we've made as we continue to progress

H.Y.P.E.
(Healing Young People through Empowerment)

"Goals Wrap-Up"

List three things you are willing to do to continue to fulfill the goals you named in Session 11:

1. _____

2. _____

3. _____

References

Allen, N. (2005). Exploring hip-hop therapy with high-risk youth. *Praxis, 5*, 30–36.

American Psychiatric Association. (2000). *Diagnostic and statistical manual of mental disorders* (4th edition, text revised). Washington, DC: Author.

Bonczar, T. P. (2003, August). Prevalence of Imprisonment in the U.S. Population, 1974-2001. Washington, DC: Bureau of Justice Statistics.

Boyd-Franklin, N. (2003). *Black families in therapy: Understanding the African-American experience* (2nd edition). New York: Guilford Press.

Caldwell, L.D. & White, J.L. (2001). African-centered therapeutic and counseling interventions for African-American males. In Brooks, G.R. & Good, G.E. (Eds.), *The new handbook of psychotherapy and counseling with men: A comprehensive guide to settings, problems, and treatment approaches, Volume Two* (pp. 737–753). San Francisco: Jossey-Bass.

Cody, P.S. (2006) Working with oppositional youths using Brief Strategic Family Therapy. In Franklin, C, Harris, M.B., & Allen-Meares, P. (Eds.), *The school services sourcebook: A guide for school-based professionals* (pp. 671–680). New York: Oxford University Press.

181

H.Y.P.E.
(Healing Young People through Empowerment)

Corbin, B.A. (1994). Helping early adolescents tell: A guided exercise for trauma-focused sexual abuse treatment groups. *Child Welfare, 73*, 141–155.

Cross, W. E., Jr. (1971). The Negro-to-Black conversion experience. *Black World, 20,* 13–27.

D'Souza, D. (1998). Racism in modern America. Retrieved May 25, 2007, from http://www.geocities.com/siliconvalley/hills/8908/rframe.htm.

Darnley-Smith, R. & Patey, H. (2003). *Music Therapy*. Thousand Oaks: Sage Publications.

Davis, L.E. (Ed.) (1999). *Working with African American males: A guide to practice.* Thousand Oaks, CA: Sage Publications.

DeCarlo, A. C. (2001). Promising practices: Rap therapy? An innovative approach to group work with urban adolescents. *Journal of Intergroup Relations, 27*, 40–49.

DeCarlo, A. & Hockman, E. (2003). RAP Therapy: A group work intervention method for urban adolescents. *Social Work with Groups, 26*, 45–59.

Deffenbacher, J. L., Lynch, R. S., Qetting, E. R., & Kemper, C. C. (1996). Anger reduction in early adolescents. *Journal of Counseling Psychology, 43,* 149–157.

References

Denham, S.A. & Almeida, M.C. (1987). Children's social problem-solving skills, behavioral adjustment, and interventions: A meta-analysis evaluating theory and practice. *Journal of Applied Developmental Psychology, 8,* 391–409.

Dubois, D. L., Holloway, B. E., Valentine, J. C., & Cooper, H. (2002). Effectiveness of mentoring programs for youth: A meta-analytical review. *American Journal of Community Psychology, 301,* 157–197.

Dyson, M.E. (1996). *Between God and gangsta rap: Bearing witness to Black culture.* New York: Oxford University Press.

Eckhohm, E. (2006, March 20). Plight deepens for Black men, studies warn. *New York Times.* Retrieved August 27, 2006 from <http://www.nytimes.org>.

Elligan, D. (2004). *Rap Therapy: A practical guide for communicating with youth and young adults through rap music.* New York: Kensington Publishing Corp.

Elligan, D. (2000). RAP Therapy: A culturally sensitive approach to psychotherapy with young African-American men. *Journal of African-American Men, 5,* 27–37.

Erik, R.R. (2004). Disruptive behavior disorders: Conduct Disorder and Oppositional Defiant Disorder. In Erik, R.R. (Ed.), *Counseling and treatment with children and adolescents with DSM-IV-T-R Disorders* (pp. 155-204). Saddle River, NJ: Pearson Education.

H.Y.P.E.
(Healing Young People through Empowerment)

Feindler, E. L. (1991). Cognitive strategies in anger-control interventions for children and adolescents. In Kendall, P. C. (Ed.), *Child and adolescent therapy: Cognitive behavioral procedures* (pp. 56-97). New York: Guilford Press.

Ford, D.Y. & Harris III, J.J. (1997). A study of the racial identity and achievement of black males and females. *Roeper Review, 20*, 105–111.

Gibbs, J.T. (2003). African-American children and adolescents. In Gibbs, J.T., Huang, L.N., & Assoc. (Eds.), *Children of color: Psychological interventions with culturally diverse youth* (pp. 95–144). San Francisco: Jossey-Bass.

Gibson, D.M. & Jefferson, R.N. (2006). The effect of perceived parental involvement and the use of growth-fostering on relationships on self-concept in adolescents participating in Gear Up. *Family Therapy, 16,* 29–43.

Gold, C., Voracek, M., & Wigram, T. (2004). Effects of music therapy for children and adolescents with psychopathology: a meta-analysis. *Journal of Child Psychology and Psychiatry, 45*, 1054–1063.

Grisso, T., Davis, M., & Vincent, G. (2004, March). Mental health and juvenile justice systems: Responding to the needs of youth with mental health conditions and delinquency. *Center for Mental Health Services Research University of Massachusetts Medical School Issue Brief, 1,* 1–3.

References

Hines, P.H. & Boyd-Franklin, N. (1996). African American Families. In McGoldrick, Giordano & Pearce (Eds.), *Ethnicity and family therapy* (2nd ed.) (pp. 66–84). New York City: The Guilford Press.

Hoke, Z. (2006). Black men lag behind in America. Retrieved August 25, 2006, from <http:// www.voanews.com/english/ archive/2006-07/Plight2006-07-15-voa.cfm?CFID=47592830& CGTOKEN=23906871>.

Indiana Education Policy Center. (2000). Zero Tolerance, Zero Evidence: An analysis of school disciplinary practice. (Policy Research Report Number SRS2).

Jackson, P. (2005, February 23). The massive failure of Black males in the American education system. *Baltimore Chronicle and Sentinel.* Retrieved July 30, 2006, from <http:// www.bridges4kids.org>.

Johnson, J.D., Jackson, L.A., & Gatto, L. (1995). Deleterious effects of exposure to rap music. *Basic and Applied Social Psychology, 16,* 27–42.

Jonson-Reid, M., Williams, J.H., & Webster, D. (2001). Severe emotional disturbance and violent offending among incarcerated adolescents. *Social Work Research, 25,* 43–50.

Joseph, J. (1999). Preventing delinquency among African-American males. Davis, L.E. (Ed.), *Working with African-American Males: A guide to practice* (259–270). Thousand Oaks, CA: Sage Publications.

H.Y.P.E.
(Healing Young People through Empowerment)

Kellner, M.H. & Bry, B.B. (1999, Winter). The effects of anger management groups in a day school for emotionally disturbed adolescents. *Adolescence, 17,* 135–145.

Kendall, P.C. & Fischler, G.L. (1984). Behavioral and adjustment correlates of problem-solving measures. *Child Development, 55,* 579–592.

King, A.E.O. (1997). Understanding violence among young A.A males: An Afrocentric perspective. *Journal of Black Studies, 28,* 79–96.

Lee, C.C. (28, February 1996). Growing pains boys to men: Adolescent Black male development. *Black Child, 23,* 24–25.

Leonard, S., Lee, C. & Kiselica, M.S. (1999). Counseling African American Male Youth. In A.M. Horne & M.S. Kiselica (Eds.) *Handbook of counseling boys and adolescent males: A practitioner's guide* (pp. 75–86). Thousand Oaks: Sage Publications.

Lipson, G.B. & Romatowski, J.A. (1983). *Ethnic Pride: Exploration into your ethnic heritage* (109–120). Carthage, IL: Good Apple Inc.

Mickel, E. & Mickel, C. (2002). Family Therapy in transition: Choice theory and music. *Journal of Reality Therapy, 11*, 37–40.

Mishel, L. & Joydeep, R. (2006). Rethinking high school graduation rates and trends. Retrieved August 12, 2006, from <http://www.epi.org/content.cfm/book_grad_rates>.

References

Nakashian, M. & Kleinman, P. (1999). Delivering comprehensive services to high-risk African-American males. Davis, L.E. (Ed.), *Working with African-American Males: A guide to practice* (259–270). Thousand Oaks, CA: Sage Publications.

National Association of School Psychologists. (n.d.). *Emotional and Behavioral Disorders.* Retrieved August 30, 2006 from <http://www.nasponline.org/information/pospaper_sebd.html>.

Nelson III, W.M., Finch Jr., A.J., and Ghee, A.C. (2006). Anger management with children and adolescents: Cognitive-Behavioral Therapy. In Kendall, P.C. (Ed.) *Child and adolescent therapy: Cognitive-behavioral procedures (3rd ed.)* (114–165). New York: The Guilford Press.

Nugent, W., Champlin, D., & Winimaki, L. (1997). The effects of anger control training on adolescent antisocial behavior. *Research on Social Work Practice, 7*, 446–462.

Office of Juvenile Justice and Delinquency Prevention. (2000). Race as a Factor in Juvenile Arrests. [Bulletin]: Pope, C. & Snyder, D. [Electronic Version] Retrieved September 1, 2005 from <http://www.ncjrs.org/pdffiles1/ojjdp/189180.pdf>.

Osher, D. & Hanley, T.V. (2001). Implementing the SED national agenda: Promising programs and policies for children and youth with emotional and behavioral problems. *Education & Treatment of Children, 24,* 374–404.

H.Y.P.E.
(Healing Young People through Empowerment)

Pajares, F. (2002). Overview of Social Cognitive Theory and of Self-Efficacy. Retrieved May 5, 2008 from <http:// www. des.emory.edu/mfp/eff.html>.

Parham, T. (2002). *Counseling persons of African decent.* Thousand Oaks: Sage.

Plummer, D. L. (1995). Patterns of racial identity development of African American adolescent males and females. *Journal of Black Psychology*, 21, 168–180.

Roderick, M. (2005). What's happening to the Boys? Early high school experiences and school outcomes among African American male adolescents in Chicago. In Fashola, O.S. (Ed.), *Education African American males: Voices from the field* (pp. 151–227). Thousand Oaks, CA: Corwin Press.

The Sentencing Project. (1999). The Crisis of the Young African-American Male and the Criminal Justice System. [Electronic Version] Washington, D.C.: Prepared for U.S. Commission on Civil Rights Retrieved September 1, 2005, from <http://www.sentencing project.org/pdfs/5022.pdf>.

Sanchez, D. & Carter, R.T. (2005). Exploring the relationship between racial identity and religious orientation among African American college students. *Journal of College Student Development, 46,* 280-295.

Sarovan, J. (1990). The use of music therapy on an adolescent psychiatric unit. *Journal of Group Psychotherapy, Psychodrama, & Sociometry, 43*, 139–142.

References

Sauders, D. (2007, July 10). Heavy time for drug lightweights. Retrieved May 25, 2008, from <http://caglepost.com/column/Deb+Sauders/4339/Heavy+Time+for+Drug+Lightweights.htm>.\

Shechtman, Z. (2003). Therapeutic factors and outcomes in group and individual therapy of aggressive boys. *Group Dynamics: Theory, Research, and Practice, 7*, 225–237.

Spivack, G. & Shure, M.B. (1974). Social adjustment of young children: A cognitive approach to solving real-life problems. San Francisco: Jossey-Bass.

Sterling, E. (n.d.). Drug laws and snitching: A primer. Retrieved May 25, 2008, from <http://www.pbs.org/wgbh/pages/frontline/shows/snitch/primer/>.

Sue, D.W. & Sue, D. (2003). Counseling the culturally diverse: Theory and practice, 4th Edition. New York: John Wiley & Sons.

Townsend, B. (2000). Disproportionate discipline of African-American children and youth: Culturally responsive strategies to reducing school suspensions and expulsions. *Exceptional Children, 66*, 381–391.

Tyson, E. H. (2002). Hip-Hop Therapy: An exploratory study of a rap music intervention with at-risk and delinquent youth. *Journal of Poetry Therapy, 15*, 133–144.

H.Y.P.E.
(Healing Young People through Empowerment)

Worrell, F., Cross, W., & Vandiver, B. (2001). Nigrescence Theory: Current status and challenges for the future. *Journal of Multicultural Counseling & Development, 29,* 201–214.

http://caglepost.com/column/Deb+Saunders/4339/Heavy+Time+for+Drug+Lightweights.html

http://en.wikipedia.org/wili/Anger

http://encarta.msn.com/dictionary_1861603873/depression.html

http://wordnet.princeton.edu/perl/webwn

http://www.answers.com/topic/sadness

http://www.azlyrics.com

http://www.cancersurvivors.org/Coping/end%20term/stages.htm

http://www.cdc.gov/nchs/data/nvsr/nvsr48/nvs48_11.pdf

http://www.children.smartlibrary.org/newinterface/segment.cfm?segment=1805

http://www.childrensdefense.org/site/DocServer/idea.pdf

References

http://www.eubios.info/biodict.htm

www.geocities.com/siliconvalley/hills/8908/rframe.htm.

http://grief.com/the-five-stages-of-grief/

www.hsp.org/default.aspx?id=397

http://www.letsgethype.com

http://www.medicinenet.com/script/main/art.asp?articlekey= 23376

http://www.medterms.com/script/main/art.asp?articlekey= 2947

www.merriam-webster.com/dictionary/atonement

http://www.ohhla.com

http://www.pbs.org/wgbh/pages/frontline/shows/snitch/ primer/

http://www.qcc.cuny.edu/SocialSciences/ppecorino/ DeathandDying_TEXT/Three-Stages-of-Grief.htm

http://www.rapworld.com/history/

www.thefreedictionary.com/atonement

H.Y.P.E.
(Healing Young People through Empowerment)

http://www.thefreedictionary.com/sadness

http://wordnetweb.princeton.edu/perl/webwn?s=anger&o2=
&o0=1&o7=&o5=&o1=1&o6=&o4=&o3=&h=
http://wordnetweb.princeton.edu/perl/webwn?s=
atonement&o2=&o0=1&o7=&o5=&o1=1&o6=&o4=&o3=&h=

http://wordnetweb.princeton.edu/perl/webwn?s=
sadness&o2=&o0=1&o7=&o5=&o1=1&o6=&o4=&o3=&h

Notes

Notes

Notes

Notes

Notes

Notes

Notes

Notes

Notes

Notes

Notes

Notes

Notes

Notes